Willie & Elaine Oliver

for your enduring friendship over the years. May God bless you with abundant grace, peace, & joy.

Love

Willie & Elaine

2/2/18

REAL
Family Talk
Answers to Questions | About Love, Marriage, and Sex

Pacific Press®
Publishing Association

Nampa, Idaho | Oshawa, Ontario, Canada
www.pacificpress.com

Cover photograph by Daniel Bedell
Inside design by Aaron Troia

Copyright © 2015 by Pacific Press® Publishing Association
Printed in the United States of America
All Rights Reserved

The authors assume full responsibility for the accuracy of all facts and quotations as cited in this book.

Unless otherwise noted, Scripture is taken from the New King James Version®. Copyright © 1982 by Thomas Nelson, Inc. Used by permission. All rights reserved.

Scripture quotations marked KJV are from the King James Version of the Bible.

Texts credited to *The Message* are from *The Message,* copyright © 1993, 1994, 1995, 1996. Used by permission of NavPress Publishing Group.

Scripture quotations marked NIV are from the HOLY BIBLE, NEW INTERNATIONAL VERSION®. Copyright © 1973, 1978, 1984, 2011 by Biblica Inc.® Used by Permission. All rights reserved worldwide.

Scripture quoted from NRSV are from the New Revised Standard Version Bible, copyright © 1989 National Council of the Churches of Christ in the United States of America. Used by permission. All rights reserved.

You can obtain additional copies of this book by calling toll-free 1-800-765-6955 or by visiting http://www.adventistbookcenter.com.

Library of Congress Cataloging-in-Publication Data:

Oliver, Willie.
 Real family talk : answers to questions about love, marriage, and sex / by Willie and Elaine Oliver.
     pages cm
 Compilation of columns from *Message* magazine's Love and Relationships column.
 ISBN 13: 978-0-8163-5728-4 (pbk.)
 ISBN 10: 0-8163-5728-5 (pbk.)
 1. Marriage—Religious aspects—Seventh-day Adventists—Miscellanea. 2. Dating (Social customs)—Religious aspects—Seventh-day Adventists—Miscellanea. 3. Sex—Religious aspects—Seventh-day Adventists—Miscellanea. I. Message (Nashville, Tenn.) II. Title.
 BV4596.M3O4115 2015
 248.4'867—dc23
                              2014044724

February 2015

Contents

Parenting

Preface

One day during the fall of 1999 I (Willie) was having lunch with Dwain Neilson Esmond in the cafeteria of the General Conference complex, at the world headquarters of the Seventh-day Adventist Church in Silver Spring, Maryland. At the time, Dwain was the associate editor of *Message* magazine, and I (Willie) the director of the Department of Family Ministries for the North American Division of the Seventh-day Adventist Church.

By the time we had consumed the nutritious and appetizing meal, we had also agreed that we (Elaine and I) would write a relationship column for *Message,* beginning with the January/February issue of 2000.

Time certainly flies. Fifteen years, dozens of columns, and three editors—Ron Smith, Washington Johnson, and Carmela Monk Crawford—later, we decided to choose from what we had written during these years, to share in a more permanent modality with an international audience who had been asking for this type of advice.

It is our hope that the information shared in this volume will serve as a catalyst to enhance your relationships, as you trust God to give you the desire and strength to honor Him in your most important daily interactions.

Warmest regards,
Willie and Elaine Oliver
Silver Spring, Maryland
realfamilytalk.hopetv.org
adventistworld.org
family.adventist.org
messagemagazine.com

Introduction

On a recent trip to Cape Town, South Africa, for meetings and a speaking appointment at a church, we were filled with joy and humility when introduced to Sipho and Thandiwe. This husband and wife duo had attended one of our presentations a few years before when we offered marriage seminars in that area. With plans in hand to divorce, Sipho and Thandiwe had attended our event out of curiosity, in addition to having promised friends they would participate. We had shared scientific findings that first-time marriages had the best chance of being successful and that every additional marriage had a higher probability for divorce. Shocked by this information, Sipho and Thandiwe had determined to use the information we provided that day to work on building a healthier and more meaningful marriage. What a joy it was to meet people whose marriage had made an about-face because of what we had shared with them.

This book is filled with counsel like the information we shared with Sipho and Thandiwe. Whether married, single, widowed, or divorced, with children or without them, you will find information to enhance all of your relationships: how to communicate with your husband so he can listen to you; when to start dating after you have been through a divorce or experienced the death of your spouse; what to do if you are experiencing abuse from your spouse; how to manage your relationship with your defiant son; how to keep your marriage alive after your children have left home; what to do for a depressed spouse; finding a mate when you have never married and are already in your thirties or older; how to forgive when your spouse has wronged you; what to do when your spouse has been unfaithful; how to respond to a boyfriend who is abusing you; and many more issues that people are dealing with in their relationships each day.

As you already know, the most challenging and, at once, the most important activity in the lives of people all over the world is to be in meaningful and happy relationships. What God meant for harmony and symphonic communication, often turns to frustration, fear, and despair.

A large part of the research literature on marriage and family processes shares that most relationships experience anguish, distress, and sorrow because of a lack of effective communication. If people learned to communicate better, they would have much more understanding between them and a foundation for building stronger and healthier relationships.

During our thirty years of marriage we have learned a lot about healthy and not so healthy relationship patterns. Much of what we know that does not work well in relationships we learned by just living with each other and noticing how poorly our relationship did when we spoke to each other or responded in certain ways. And, of course, much of what we know that works well in relationships is because of the many years of studying formally and informally and being trained to practice skills and techniques that are helpful for developing excellent relationships. To be sure, we have learned to use those skills ourselves, which is one of the reasons we are still married to each other. Having wonderful relationships does not happen by chance or in a vacuum. We must invest time, effort, and interest for our relationships to grow healthier and remain viable.

Being in relationship with others is a wonderful part of God's original and perfect design for the human race from the creation of the world. The challenge is that human beings were perfect at the time marriage was invented by the Creator. However, as soon as Adam and Eve sinned, the first thing to go was that incredible feeling of oneness, of being on the same team that they had experienced thus far. Adam blamed Eve for eating the forbidden fruit (Genesis 3:12), and Eve blamed the serpent for making her forget God's clear instructions and expectations (verse 13).

We are not suggesting here that marriage, parenting, and other important relationships work only in perfect environments. Rather, our objective in answering the questions in the pages that follow is to accentuate the need to live with the reality of imperfection and to communicate that we can learn to listen and speak to each other in ways that facilitate growth and happiness.

To remain married, to parent our children without hurting them or having them drive us insane, or to be engaged in any other kind of meaningful relationship, we should know ahead of time that there will be bumps along the way. As we speak with each other, we must keep our expectations in perspective. The more aware we are of the reality that unpleasant situations will emerge in our relationships, the more likely we will be to handle difficult issues in a more calm and effective way.

Our marriage and family has not been perfect. We often share with our audiences around the world that there are no perfect marriages, families, or relationships because there are no perfect people. Perfection, nevertheless, is not the goal of relationships on earth. Commitment, a positive attitude, and striving to grow together daily are more realistic ideals for navigating the relationships that really count in our lives each day.

Being intentional about connecting and creating a positive and safe environment for the people we are in relationships with is what makes marriage, family, and relationships a worthy and worthwhile venture. Such is not possible without the power and help of our heavenly Father. With God on our side we cannot fail (Philippians 4:13). It is this kind of relationship that makes for happy and productive people who contribute to the well-being of the home, the church, and societies all over the world.

It is our hope that the stories featured in this book will be of help to you in all the important relationships of your life. After all, when there is joy in our relationships we are more likely to convey to others that we are truly disciples of Jesus Christ (John 13:35).

Marriage

Awfully Wedded

My husband and I don't have a very good marriage. The first few months after our wedding we had a lot of fun and got along quite well. Since then, things have gone south. We seem to disagree with each other in every conversation, and since the children arrived—we have two boys—it has just added to the stress in our marriage, and our lack of peaceful conversations with each other. If things don't get better soon between us, I may not be able to stay in this marriage much longer. Please help! We can't talk to each other anymore.

E ffective communication is essential to the survival of every marriage. If we were to look at marriage as a living organism, good communication would be like healthy blood running through every cell in the system to remain viable. And if marriage were a car engine, good communication would be like oil with enough viscosity to keep the parts well lubricated in order to function well.

One of the greatest challenges in married life—once the honeymoon is over—is for couples to engage in frequent conversation that is calm, civil, constructive, affirming, peaceful, and understanding. It is a delusion to believe getting along well before marriage means you will continue to do so after marriage. It is amazing how much stress, tension, and trouble a few dishes that need washing, bills that need paying, floors that need sweeping, and babies who need feeding can bring to an otherwise wonderful and blissful marriage.

Good communication is not a skill we often bring to marriage. Most of us came up in families in which voices were raised—sometimes more than just a little—when people disagreed with each other. This unfortunate legacy must be discarded to survive the rigors of real life in marriage.

There are two elements that are particularly important to having good communication in marriage, or any other meaningful relationship: making it clear and making it safe.

Quite frequently lack of clarity causes miscommunication in marriage. Many of the most heated arguments take place because a husband or wife failed to understand what his or her spouse meant to say, making things very unclear and leaving spouses very angry at each other.

Having a great marriage means that both husband and wife should be able to express their feelings, beliefs, concerns, and preferences clearly without damaging the relationship in the process. For this to happen, each spouse must feel safe to share what is on his or her mind, which can be accomplished only in an environment in which each spouse is careful about not hurting the feelings of the other.

To accomplish these two important concepts that are essential to great communication, there should be an agreement to (1) listen first and talk second. (2) Resist the urge to defend yourself. (3) Paraphrase what your spouse is saying to make sure you understand each other and are on the same page. (4) Share the process so you both have an opportunity to listen and speak to each other. (5) Pray for patience, a willing heart to resolve your differences to satisfaction, and a desire to give honor and glory to God in the process.

The Bible states in Proverbs 25:11: "A word fitly spoken is like apples of gold in settings of silver." Determine that every time you speak to your spouse it will be like giving him a gift of gold and silver, so your conversation with each other will find new joy and peace, and be a blessing to your children and their children.

How to Cope With Mental Illness in the Family

A few months ago my husband of ten years had a mental breakdown and attempted to commit suicide. He was committed to a psychiatric hospital and diagnosed with bipolar disorder. I always expected marriage to be challenging and was prepared to deal with that, but nothing prepared me to deal with a spouse with mental illness. I'm struggling with whether or not to leave him. I want my kids and me to be safe. What should I do?

While you are the only person who can ultimately decide how to handle your present situation, we hope the following information will guide you in making the decision that is best for you and your family.

Mental illness can be a devastating stressor for any marriage or family. For too long, mental illness has been the "silent" illness in many faith communities. Unfortunately, this silence has caused many to go undiagnosed and untreated, and has left family members unprepared to deal with a very real, and sometimes destructive, illness.

When a family member is diagnosed with a lifelong, life-threatening illness, it can scare a spouse away or leave parents and other family members in distress. According to the article "Managing Bipolar Disorder" in the November 2003 *Psychology Today,* in marriages in which a person has bipolar disorder it is estimated that 90 percent of these marriages end in divorce. Studies suggest that nearly half of the people living with bipolar disorder attempt killing themselves. The unpredictability and instability of volatile emotions of someone with mental illness can lead to insecurity and fragility in the marriage and the family.

In spite of daunting statistics, many marriages and families have survived living with a spouse or family member with mental illness. Recently it has become far too common for people to say of someone who is behaving strangely, "Oh, that person is bipolar." Most people would not easily recognize signs of mental illness, and just because someone is a little moody may not necessarily mean he is bipolar. What is important is to identify if a spouse, child, or other loved one behaves in erratic and unpredictable ways that create a lot of tension and instability in the family. When you identify such disruptions, getting help from a professional counselor, psychologist, or psychiatrist is critical.

Early intervention and proper diagnosis and treatment are important first steps in managing mental illness. As a supporting spouse or caregiver, educate yourself as much as possible on the person's illness. Spouses and families must also develop coping strategies and safety plans for the person with the illness and for the rest of the family. For someone who has attempted suicide and survived, it may take weeks, and maybe even months, before medication and therapy reduce his suicidal feelings. Empathy, kindness, and support from loved ones are a valuable part of treatment. Of course, this may be extremely difficult for loved ones who are confused, frightened, and angry themselves. Learning to cope with both the behavior of the mentally ill person and one's own reactions to that behavior often requires counseling for a spouse and the rest of the family as well.

One huge advantage for the Christian who is living with a mentally ill relative is faith in God. Recent studies have affirmed that a person's faith plays an important role in helping such an individual cope with challenges in his or her life—including helping family members cope with the stress of caring for a mentally ill relative. However, this faith has to be intrinsic, rather than extrinsic; meaning, the person must truly believe what he or she claims to believe. "I can do all things through Christ who strengthens me" (Philippians 4:13).

We hope our response will help you and others in similar circumstances. Beyond that, always remember the promise of God in Isaiah 41:10, "Fear not, for I am with you; be not dismayed, for I am your God. I will strengthen you, yes, I will help you, I will uphold you with My righteous right hand."

Making Differences Work

I am an introvert, and my wife an extrovert. I like to spend time with her but also like to read and spend time quietly. She likes to talk all the time. When we do things my way, she feels lonely and abandoned. When we do things her way, I feel drained. How can we meet both of our needs and feel good about each other?

Your question is thoughtful and timely. What is remarkable about your situation is that you and your wife made it through dating and actually decided to get married despite the obvious differences you see now. What happened? This is the question many couples are asking. What was special when you dated that made you overlook these significant differences? Why is it a concern now?

The truth is, your dilemma is very common in marriage. When you are dating, opposites attract. However, in marriage we tend to be much more honest with ourselves, knowing that our situation is meant to be for life. Here is where the differences are no longer attractive; they become annoying, and we are not as quick to overlook them.

To some degree this happens to every couple, because we all have different temperaments. In psychology the notion identified as temperament is that part of a person's disposition that they were born with, which makes them an introvert or an extrovert. Essentially, this is what is going on with you and your wife. You are naturally different. You don't behave that way on purpose to annoy the other; it is the way you both instinctively behave.

Now that you are married and life has set in, your respective temperaments have become much more noticeable to each other. Now that the chase is over—which often makes us too excited to notice the differences—and you have come down from cloud nine, which is much more real in relationships than we realize, you can actually notice the differences.

In order to remain happy and satisfied in your marriage, you and your wife need to sit down and talk openly about your differences, preferably with a good marriage counselor if your relationship has deteriorated to the point you can only shout and scream about this matter. Acknowledge your differences, and decide how you are going to manage them. "With God all things are possible" (Matthew 19:26).

Because you love and are committed to each other, you can make this work. Marriage behaves like everything else in life: you have to conquer the rough spots to really enjoy what is important in what you are involved in. Also, find strength in the reality that married couples all over the world have also experienced what you are going through.

Thank God for your spouse, and by His strength allow Him to use these differences to help you grow stronger in your faith, and in your love for each other.

Let's Talk, Please

My husband never wants to talk about any subject that causes conflict. I can change myself, but I can't solve our problems by myself. What do you suggest?

Understanding that you can change only yourself puts you in a unique place to do well in relationships. Most people waste much energy and time trying to change their mate, only to be utterly disappointed with the reality that there is nothing they can do to make that happen. On the other hand, we feel your frustration about wanting to clear the air about issues in your relationship while thinking your husband has no interest.

Ask yourself why your husband seems reluctant to talk about issues you often disagree about. Is it possible that when you are not getting along, there are bad feelings between you for a long time? Or, perhaps, when you speak about disagreements your conversation tends to escalate out of control, and you say things you later regret that further distance you from each other? Most men want to have peace at home, avoiding any kind of "drama" at all cost.

From the beginning of time, our ancestors—Adam and Eve—were fearful of dealing with differences. This is the reason they covered themselves when they first sinned. They concealed those parts of their bodies that were the most different. Little did they know, those differences were the very places God wanted them to find the greatest joy. As fallen humans we have inherited this legacy from our first parents, and continue to encounter challenges in this area. Managing differences is the most challenging reality in marriage.

The truth is, when a married couple takes the time to talk about their differences (conflicts) in a controlled and calm way, the results are often outstanding. In order for this to happen, couples need to learn to communicate effectively—not an easy task, even for the best of us. As a rule we tend to believe we are right and our mate is wrong. This is the reason we get upset, making it very difficult to talk to each other in a kind and gentle voice.

Make up your mind that you will approach areas of conflict in your marriage in a calm and agreeable way. Start with issues that are pretty simple, those you can handle relatively easily. When you solve these seemingly insignificant differences, your marriage relationship will experience greater intimacy. The more closeness you experience with your husband, the easier it will be for him to talk with you about other areas of conflict. The more you clear the air between you, the stronger and more satisfying your relationship will become, creating an environment of greater trust and openness to deal with more issues.

This approach will not solve your problems overnight. However, the more patience you exercise, the more successful and rewarding your marital relationship will be. When you create this kind of home environment, you will be a blessing to your children, to your neighbors, and to your friends. This is very difficult to do. Ask God for the strength (Matthew 7:7), and you will be victorious.

We hope you and your husband will experience greater peace and a renewed marriage relationship. We are praying for you.

Life After an Empty Nest

When you become empty nesters, how do you keep or reignite the spark in your marriage?

The level of health of every marriage relationship is based on the habits the spouses practice toward each other on a consistent basis. If a husband and wife are kind, understanding, patient, spiritual, nice, dependable, honest, thoughtful, forgiving, helpful, and make their marriage relationship a priority, marriage will be a little heaven on earth. The opposite is also true. By being irritable, impatient, sarcastic, unforgiving, selfish, dishonest, undependable, mean, spiteful, cruel, disconnected, and not making marriage their priority relationship, this type of marriage will become conflicted and devitalized.

What is commonly known as empty-nest syndrome is a sensation of loneliness felt by parents or other adult caretakers (guardians, grandparents, aunts, uncles, and so on) when one or more of their children leave home to go to school, get married, or simply move out on their own. While these feelings of loneliness are more likely to be experienced by women, men often experience them as well. These feelings develop when parents feel they are becoming less influential in the lives of their children, while the authority or influence of others (professors, spouses, friends, and so on) seems to be growing.

It is essential for married men and women to understand that marriage needs to be the primary relationship in their lives. As much as one loves one's mother and/or father, when one gets married, the spouse becomes the highest priority relationship after God. This is not our opinion; it is God's directive. In Genesis 2:24, God says, "Therefore a man shall leave his father and mother and be joined to his wife, and they shall become one flesh." This means marriage is the only relationship under the sun in which we get to become one with another person. We cannot (must not) become one with our son or daughter; that oneness is reserved for only our spouse.

When children are born to a married couple there is a tendency for the child (or children) to become the focus of primary attention. Because babies are helpless and need the attentiveness of responsible adults to survive and thrive, we have the predisposition to go overboard and become careless with each other. If husband or wife feels justified in taking this approach the marriage relationship will take a back seat and naturally deteriorate. If not caught early, this pattern may continue until the child or children leave home, rendering marriage a distant, often cold, and spark-free relationship.

If you are married and still child free, follow the counsel we gave in the first paragraph by being intentional about making your spouse your priority relationship, even when children come. If you follow this course, when your children leave home you will still have each other for support, love, and affection, and the spark will still be in your marriage. If you have done differently, have a serious conversation with your spouse about the reality of your marital relationship. Ask your spouse for forgiveness, then find a good Christian counselor who can help you talk through the hurt and pain of the past in order to get a new perspective on the type of marriage you want to have. Dealing with this matter with the help of the right professional will clear the way to reignite the spark you once had.

Trust God to develop the kind of marriage relationship He meant for you to have. We are praying for you.

A Preview of Reality

I just got married two months ago to my on-again, off-again boyfriend of six years. During our dating we often argued about his computer game habit. I thought that when we got married it would change. But it's the same, and it has gotten even worse. Since he hasn't finished college, I enrolled him in an online course last year, with his consent, but until now he has not completed one lesson. I thought that he would study now that we are married, but his attitude toward studying is still the same as it was before we got married. We have worship frequently for about fifteen minutes each time, he then rushes to continue his online games until he gets tired. I don't know what to do for him to minimize his playing online games. It is gradually wrecking our marriage. I am trying to understand him but just don't know how. My husband is thirty-four and I am thirty-two. Please help me to work out this marriage.

We were saddened to hear your story but pleased that you reached out to us. Like you, many young adults make the mistake of marrying someone who has glaring flaws they think will disappear after marriage. Most people do not change very much after marriage. Like your husband, men who played video games incessantly before marriage invariably continue that behavior after marriage. The same is true about their interest or lack of interest in school or work. The best predictor of what your mate will be like after marriage is what your mate is like before marriage. You must realize that you cannot be your husband's mother and that you cannot change him. You cannot decide it is time for him to finish school, or for him to work longer hours, or for him to quit playing video games. These habits will change only if your husband determines he wants to change. You have absolutely no power to change your husband.

We suggest you take this matter to the Lord in prayer. Jesus is the Prince of Peace. Ask Him to help you change your attitude and the way you approach your husband. Since you chose to marry him, love him unconditionally and accept him for who he is. Once your husband feels accepted it will be much easier to speak with him and encourage him to get professional help.

Claim God's promise never to leave you alone (Matthew 28:20), to keep you in perfect peace (John 14:27), and to supply all your needs (Philippians 4:19). You will continue to be in our prayers.

, Who Me?

...ays talks about me not being submissive to him, as well as him being head of the household. What does it mean for the wife to be submissive as the Bible says?

T he answer to your question is rather simple, but difficult to believe because we usually approach Scripture with preconceived notions. Rather than taking the Bible for what it says, we often bring our own frames of reference—our culture, the way we were raised, and our own opinions.

The Bible reference for your husband's comment is Ephesians 5:22–24: "Wives, submit to your own husbands, as to the Lord. For the husband is head of the wife, as also Christ is head of the church; and He is the Savior of the body. Therefore, just as the church is subject to Christ, so let the wives be to their own husbands in everything."

We happen to agree with the Bible reference. However, the Bible says more in verses 25–28: "Husbands, love your wives, just as Christ also loved the church and gave Himself for her . . . that He might present her to Himself a glorious church, not having spot or wrinkle or any such thing, but that it should be holy and without blemish. So husbands ought to love their own wives as their own bodies; he who loves his wife loves himself." We also believe these words. As you see, the passage is a directive for a wonderful life between husbands and wives. Wives have responsibilities, and husbands do as well. The peak of this refrain is found in verse 33: "Nevertheless let each one of you in particular so love his own wife as himself, and let the wife see that she respects her husband."

Obviously Paul is writing to Christians in the church at Ephesus and is making a point about harmony between husbands and wives. To do justice to our response, we must go back to the statement in verse 21: "Submitting to one another in the fear of God." This verse is like an abstract or thesis statement for the remaining twelve verses. Before developing his sayings, Paul summarizes what he is about to share in greater detail. Paul's bottom line is mutual submission. So even before addressing wives to submit, Paul urges husbands and wives to submit to each other in the fear of God. Another version says, "out of reverence for Christ" (NIV).

Jesus taught His disciples not to try to become great at someone else's expense, or to throw their weight around because they were in His inner circle. As you know, the disciples failed the lesson. Even while Jesus ate His last meal with them, they argued over which of them was the greatest (Luke 22:24–27). Then Jesus washed the feet of His disciples to teach them by modeling that whoever uses his authority to build up people, rather than the one who simply wants to build up his own authority—like the Pharisees—is the greatest.

One way to know someone is head of the home is not because the person says so, but because the person serves more. The person loves as Jesus loves—unconditionally—and puts others first (Romans 12:10; Philippians 2:1–4). Our human nature is egotistical and leads us to promote ourselves. When you are filled with the Spirit of God, you can love as Jesus loves, and submission in that environment is simply a response to love.

We hope you and your husband will be submissive to Jesus. When Christ is in control of your lives, submission, love, and respect will be the practice in your home.

A Cure for Nagging

My husband has a habit that I disapprove of. How can I help him quit without being a nagging wife?

All human beings have bad habits. We have said before that there are no perfect marriages because there are no perfect people. We all come to marriage as products of our respective backgrounds. Our behavior as adults has much to do with where, how, and by whom we were brought up.

You will need to make the distinction in your mind if the disapproving habit of your husband's is a sinful one that is destroying your marriage and family or simply a habit that annoys you to no end. Either way, your approach and attitude will determine, to a great extent, whether you can solve the situation or make matters worse.

The truth is you cannot change your husband. Married people often lose sleep thinking about how much they would like to see certain habits in their spouses disappear. To be sure, your husband's disapproving habit is not in your circle of control. The way you determine to relate to this habit, however, is in your circle of control.

You can help your husband quit his bad habit only if you are friends and are having fun together on a regular basis. The more fun you have together as a couple, the easier it will be to deal with the negative issues in your relationship. If you do not have fun with your husband you are not in a position to help him change.

So here is what you can do to deal with this matter without being a nagging wife and having a good chance of changing things around:

1. Tell your husband that you have been thinking of ways that you can build time into your weekly routine to have more fun together. Invite him to sit with you and individually make a list of fun things you can do together. Pick three or four things from the list you would enjoy doing and schedule time to do them together.

2. Once you start having fun on a regular basis, invite your husband to set aside time each week to have a meeting in which you can talk about things in your marriage that you are pleased about, and things you have concerns about. Take turns sharing your feelings and make it as pleasant as possible by using "I" messages when sharing your concern. For example, "I feel taken for granted when you stay at work late, and you don't call me to let me know you will be home late." Do not start by accusing him of never calling you. Rather tell him in a nonthreatening way by using "I" messages.

When you have fun together, you create a positive environment in your marriage that increases your willingness to bring up concerns and solve your problems. The more you solve your problems, the more positive your marriage becomes, which increases your wish to have more fun together.

Take the time to enjoy the good things in your marriage, creating a positive environment in which to bring up important concerns and being able to solve them.

Kindness and Compassion Are Key

We say couples have to have total honesty to survive, but husbands cannot be totally honest. A wife can tell a husband he needs to lose weight and he is getting fat. Husbands can never tell a wife that she is getting fat. What do you think about this?

One of the most important elements of any strong and healthy marriage—or any other important human relationship for that matter—is honesty. We often hear the adage that honesty is the best policy; we could not agree more.

It is also true that for relationships to thrive, we need to know how best to communicate the truth for maximum and positive results. Any fool can say the first thing that comes to mind. However, the careful, cautious, and sensible person edits her thoughts to affirm, nurture, and safeguard the relationship that is so valuable to her.

All of us—men and women—arrive at adulthood with baggage. We are all products of our families of origin. However and wherever we were brought up, we are who we are because of the interactions—positive or negative—that took place around us and with us when we were growing up. All of us are wounded to some extent, and it does not take much for us to be hurt pretty badly if someone targets our weak or vulnerable spots.

Our work in relationships is to help each other grow toward health: emotional, intellectual, spiritual, physical, and even financial. To accomplish this goal we must follow the counsel found in Philippians 4:8, which states: "Finally, brethren, whatsoever things are true, whatsoever things are honest, whatsoever things are just, whatsoever things are pure, whatsoever things are lovely, whatsoever things are of good report; if there be any virtue, and if there be any praise, think on these things" (KJV).

We do not believe women should say hurtful things to their husbands any more than men should say hurtful things to their wives. While we should concentrate on speaking the truth, we should do it in a noble or gracious manner.

We cannot imagine speaking the truth as the apostle Paul suggests and offend one's spouse at the same time. To speak the truth is much more than just being honest; it is being kind, compassionate, and downright great company. In marriage we must resist the urge to keep it real, as often urged by the contemporary urban maxim of sharing unvarnished truth. It is a fallacy that to tell the truth we must be ugly, rough, and crass.

Your question sounds like that of a man who actually feels hurt and slighted by what his wife has said to him about his weight. You seem to be suffering in silence because to do otherwise may suggest that you are less than a man or simply too delicate to be a man. However, it is probably time for you to accept your hurt head-on and share with your wife in a kind and nonthreatening way how you feel about what she often says to you about your weight.

American culture is quite unkind to people who carry weight beyond that which is socially accepted. And while most people could lose weight if they ate less and exercised for thirty minutes each day, it is not as easily done as it is easily said. Because food is very enjoyable, we often overdo it to make ourselves feel better when other areas of our lives are not going as well as we wished they were.

You are wise to think that it may not be a good idea to tell your wife that she is fat and needs to lose weight. If she is truly fat, or thinks she is fat, she already knows that. What she does need from you is to help make her burdens light by being kind, compassionate, courteous, and a husband who loves unconditionally and is in the marriage for the long haul.

We hope you will always choose to tell the truth in a style that will build up your mate and relationship.

Married Couples and Depression

My husband has suffered with depression for most of our marriage. I love him very much and hate to see him suffer; however, it's becoming increasingly difficult for me to deal with his "sadness." Sometimes, I feel like I just can't live like this anymore. I want to stay married, but I also want to be happy.

Depression touches the lives of many individuals at some time during the life span. Sometimes it is just a temporary mood, but on other occasions the condition may lead to suicidal psychosis. No one is exempt, not even in a normally loving and happy marriage.

It is critical for couples to know how to handle depression. Marriage researchers who have studied the effects of depression on marriage have found that when depression is present in one or both spouses, communication deteriorates. When communication breaks down, conflict increases and much of the joy of marriage may diminish or disappear. To be sure, many couples may divorce if this condition is left unchecked.

Being concerned about your husband's condition is a good thing. If your husband's condition is more than just a fleeting "feeling down" mood, given your statement about his depression for most of your marriage, you may want to encourage him to visit his primary care physician as soon as possible. Getting a complete physical is a good place to begin, since his physician will ask him a battery of questions regarding his emotional well-being. Sometimes, as depression worsens, the loss of energy is accompanied by sleep problems, loss of appetite or excessive eating, withdrawal from social activities, extreme sadness and pessimism, and/or an inability to enjoy pleasurable events. If several of these symptoms are present, the physician will refer your husband to a psychiatrist or other mental health professional.

When depression occurs in a spouse, it is very tempting for the other spouse to become impatient, critical, frustrated, and even angry. Resist the urge to tell your husband to "snap out of it." Usually when someone becomes depressed, whatever the cause—chemical imbalance or psychological trauma—he usually is not capable of just changing his attitude and moving on quickly. We recommend that you both seek individual and couple counseling. The spouse who is not depressed needs to seek counseling as well so that he may better cope with his partner's depression.

This is also a good time to step up your prayer life individually and together as a couple. Prayer does change things, but mostly it changes us. Pray and ask God to heal your husband's depression and to give you the strength and patience you need during the healing process. Because it may be difficult for your spouse to communicate his needs during his depression, you will need to anticipate his need for love and support. Ask God to give you the strength to love him unconditionally, as 1 Corinthians 13 teaches. Look for opportunities to encourage him, reassure him of your love, and give him warm hugs.

We pray you and your husband will allow God to work in you and through you, and that you both will heed the counselors' advice that will likely lead to your growing closer together and finding healing for your relationship and the depression.

Growing Apart

My husband and I have been married for about ten years and have three small children. The children and work take up quite a bit of my time and energies. On the other hand, my husband seems to be working all the time— at his job, at home, or at church. Over the years something has changed in our relationship, and I don't believe it is for the better. I feel that we are growing apart. What can we do to change that? I am afraid that if we continue the way we are going, we soon won't have a marriage. Please help.

A dangerous reality in marriage is that not long after the wedding every couple will find their relationship heading for trouble. This does not happen once in a while. Trouble takes place all the time, and will overcome every marriage unless the husband and wife have made up their minds that they will take proven steps to prevent this trouble from destroying their marriage.

While it is common to believe that every couple wants to be happy, reality is that the happiness in marriage begins to disappear for most couples within a few weeks or months after the wedding. Why is it so difficult to keep it together in marriage? Dating is fun, but marriage seems to be a drag. Why? Because of what you have described above.

Before marriage, couples cannot wait to see each other at the end of the day or on weekends. They live to have fun with each other and enjoy it so much that if they get married—so they never have to be apart again—they believe their happiness will always be present. But then real life sets in—work, commuting, dishes, laundry, rent or mortgage, children, church work, PTA, in-laws, and so on—and there goes the neighborhood. You are so busy at work all day, and with the house and children when you get home in the evenings, that there is no time to scratch your head or to even think. And to make matters worse, your husband seems to be involved at work or at church most of the time so that when he finally gets home, you have no time or energy to deal with each other.

What can you do to change things around? The secret to a happy marriage, which many believe is still a secret, is friendship and commitment. So in order to prevent the slide down the slippery slope you are describing above, you need to know that the only marriages that survive and thrive are the ones in which the marriage partners are friends and are committed to doing what it takes to make their marriage work.

We suggest, then, that to keep your marriage alive and vibrant you must be committed to having fun together, just the two of you, on a regular basis. At least once a week, for an hour or two, you need to spend time enjoying each other. Go for a walk, or go out to eat, or visit a museum, or listen to music that you both enjoy, or read a book together, or take a weekend break, just the two of you. This is hard to do, couples tell us all the time. We know. It has been hard for us as well. However, it is much harder to be in an unhappy and unfulfilling marriage when you have allowed the busyness of life to make you strangers. It is much more difficult to be in a marriage in which you feel disconnected, and are constantly dealing with problems, arguing about money, the children, or where to go to church.

The reality is that there will always be conflicts in marriage that you will need to talk about, manage, and solve. Until your kids are grown and have left home you will always be busy with their issues. However, if you make friendship in your marriage a priority by spending time together, protecting that friendship time from talking about problems, and practicing to talk like friends—not judging each other, or criticizing each other, but listening to each other's goals and dreams or silly stories, your marriage will be a different and a more pleasant place to be. And when you are happy with each other, and feel good about each other, dealing with the problems that will come up in marriage will be much easier to handle because you trust and like each other.

We hope you will be committed to making the time for friendship in your marriage, and will trust God for patience, forgiveness, and commitment in your marriage.

Unhappily Married

I never thought this would happen to me, but I find myself very unhappy in my marriage. My wife and I just don't communicate well, and when we do, we yell at each other and there is a lot of tension between us. We don't seem to be compatible and have very few interests in common. How can such a dysfunctional relationship survive? This cannot possibly be healthy for our children. I don't believe God expects me to stay in such an unhappy relationship. What do you think?

We are sorry to hear about your frustration and pain, but we are pleased to tell you that your condition does not have to be permanent or terminal. In fact, there are not many—if any—married couples alive or dead, who have not experienced or are experiencing what you have just described.

The reality about relationships is that "opposites attract" during the dating period, but this is not especially true about marriage. When it comes to marriage, we want to be married to ourselves. In other words, we want our spouse to like the foods that we like and to want to eat them on the same days we feel like eating them. We also want our spouse to like to do the activities we like to do, to like the television programs we like—including football, basketball, and baseball in season. The one thing we want our spouse to be different about is to not want to buy expensive shoes on the same month we have bought expensive shoes. We buy shoes only when we really need them and always use good judgment, but when our spouse buys shoes, she always does so emotionally and could have waited a few months or didn't have to buy such an expensive pair. Actually, we would rather that she never bought expensive shoes, even if they cost half of what our shoes cost, because we need to be careful with our spending since we are saving for a down payment on our first home.

Unfortunately, most of us who are married will experience the tension that comes from living with a spouse who has different expectations about almost everything. And because we live such fast-paced lives, we often make no time to sit together to coordinate what needs to happen so that our lives are lived on the same page. Of course, our lack of planning leaves us to make assumptions about many things, and when our assumptions are incorrect or don't come to pass—as usually happens with assumptions—we are upset with the person who sabotaged them. And when this happens day in and day out, we become frustrated, good feelings take wings, and we feel as you have expressed in your statement above.

We believe you can change what's going on in your marriage by making the following alterations:

- Change your attitude and expectations about your marriage.
- Admit that there is no perfect relationship because there are no perfect people.
- Be intentional about doing something for your spouse every day that communicates she is precious to you.
- Ask yourself what you can do differently to bring happiness into your home and do something about it.
- Make some time every week just to have fun with your spouse.
- Make the time every week to talk about your schedules and be sure to share with your spouse anything that will be different than your regular schedule.
- Be quick to apologize for causing pain to your spouse whether what you did was on purpose or by mistake.

Commit yourself to having a positive attitude about your marriage and doing all you can to implement that change. If there is no change after following what we have suggested, please make sure you and your spouse get help from a Christian counselor or pastor. We are praying for you.

Early Marital Conflict Management

We have been married for just a few months, and this amazing experience is nothing either of us could imagine. We've had a ball being married. We haven't had any major problems so far. But repeatedly I am hurting his feelings by what he describes to me as ignoring him. This occurs when we are out together and I do something inadvertently that doesn't consider him. I usually find out in the aftermath when he's sulking or not talking to me. I want to convey that I do appreciate him and that I do not take him for granted. I want to be aware of his every feeling. How can I gauge it to know when I am hurting him and when I am not?

We read your note with delight. It is great to hear a newly married person express joy in the marriage experience as you have. We are also pleased to know that despite having such a good time, you have expressed a commitment to handling conflict in your marriage early, before the situation gets out of hand.

What you have described above is not unusual in marriage, especially in a marriage that is as recent as yours. Conflict is natural and inevitable in all relationships, especially marriage. People in relationships are going to have differences in the way they relate to certain behaviors because of their families of origin (where they grew up), their experiences with others, and the type of temperament or personality they have. Some people are outgoing and the life of the party (you seem to be this type) and are called sanguine; others are more introspective, reserved, and moody (your husband seems to be this type) and are called melancholic.

The more you learn about personality types, the more you will understand each other, and the easier it will be to manage the conflict that arises when your husband is hurt by the way you behave. It is important for you to make the time at regular intervals to share with each other your likes and dislikes in a nonthreatening environment. The more you talk and understand each other, the easier it will be to handle misunderstandings.

Since neither you nor your husband is perfect, you can be sure that each of you will either do things or say things that will hurt the other inadvertently. However, you need to assure each other that you love each other, want to make each other happy, and will never do anything on purpose to hurt the other. When something is done or not done, said or not said, that makes the other unhappy, you already know that it is not being done on purpose.

You should continue to express your love and appreciation for your husband. However, there is little you can do to make sure you never take your husband for granted. There will be times that your husband will feel taken for granted despite the fact that it was not your intention to do so. Much of this reality has to do with the differences between your personalities. When this happens, you need to apologize and reassure him that it was not your intention to hurt him. You may also continue to learn his ways and keep in mind what will make him happy and what will make him unhappy, and behave accordingly.

On the other hand, we hope that when your husband feels hurt, he will tell you kindly rather than expecting you to notice his silence or his sulking. You cannot read your husband's mind and should not be expected to. As for your desire to be aware of your husband's every feeling, it probably will never happen. It is not your responsibility to gauge whether you have hurt your husband or not. It is his responsibility to share his feelings with you, and your responsibility to be kind and responsive.

It is our hope you will plan to share your feelings with each other openly and often, so that you each will grow in your knowledge and love of each other, and in your commitment to each other. Trust God and remember that with Him all things are possible.

Is Divorce an Option?

My husband does not communicate very much. He doesn't even like it when I speak on the phone too much. And he really gets mad when we are having dinner and I answer the phone. What if someone is dying or really needs to reach me? I am responsible for several things at my church, and people need to reach me. What do you think I should do?

Men and women are different. And they often communicate differently as well. There is an impression in Western culture that, on average, women talk much more than men do and are more relational by nature. However, the fact that a man may not speak as much as his wife doesn't mean that he is not communicating. Communication experts suggest that only 7 percent of communication is based on the actual words a person is using in conversation. Other elements of communication may include tone of voice and body language. This, of course, means that your husband may very well be communicating even if he is not saying anything.

Our own observation and experience is that women usually speak on the telephone much more than men do. This isn't good or bad, but simply different.

In marriage it is important for couples to talk about and come to an agreement on the expectations they have for each other. Couples need to communicate on how to spend time together when they get home at the end of the day. Lack of familiarity with each other's expectations is half of the battle you have described above.

It is also important for married couples to talk about and develop a phone etiquette that communicates respect and regard for each other. If a husband or wife spends most of the time they are at home with each other speaking to someone else on the telephone, that behavior may communicate a lack of interest in connecting with each other. Again, reasonable boundaries need to be set.

Agree to turn off the telephone during dinner or to simply not answer the telephone at that time. When a person takes a telephone call during dinnertime, what is often innocently communicated is that the person on the other side of the conversation—whoever that may be—is more important than they are. Most of these calls are probably made by telemarketers who are selling products we are not interested in. And yet we have just hurt the closest and dearest people to us.

Even pastors, physicians, and others in the helping professions need to develop healthy boundaries about telephone use when they are at home with their families or risk becoming disconnected and distant from their spouse, children, and other loved ones. While helping others is important, charity begins at home. And unless we demonstrate love and respect for those we live with, trying to save the rest of the world can be futile and somewhat hypocritical.

It is our hope you will give serious thought to what we have shared and determine through God's power to have a happier and more peaceful marriage.

Where Has the Romance Gone?

My husband used to be very romantic, sending me cards, flowers, and so on. I don't remember the last time I got something special from him. How can I jump-start the romantic relationship we once had?

The truth about relationships is that the more familiar we are with someone the less attentive we tend to be. At the beginning of most relationships, during the courtship phase, couples tend to work harder to express their love and admiration for one another. However, it seems that once the vows are said or shortly afterward, one or both partners settle into a mode of taking the other for granted. Couples today spend much of their time devoted to their careers, homes, cars, and individual leisure. While these pursuits are not inherently bad, if they command too much of their time, there will be much disenchantment and dissatisfaction with the marriage.

Nevertheless, let's not confuse love with the expression of love. Every marriage needs to be based on a decision to love regardless of feelings. Love is a decision. The love that builds a marriage is agape love—the kind of love that God has for us. Agape love is being more concerned with the good of the other person. Agape love loves the other person in spite of, not because of, who they are. Yet, true love must not allow itself to grow cold.

You can take the lead in jump-starting the relationship; your husband may not be aware that something is wrong. Perhaps you can start by doing something romantic for your husband. Spend time just enjoying each other's company. Let him know how much you enjoy spending time with him and that you are committed to keeping the sparks alive in your marriage. Let him know how much you love to receive flowers, cards, and other little niceties from him. Don't accuse, blame, or attack him for not doing these things for you; remember to use "I" statements (e.g., "Honey, I enjoy it when . . .").

Author Ellen White says succinctly in *Happiness Homemade,* "Determine to be all that is possible to be to each other. Continue the early attentions . . . then marriage, instead of being the end of love, will be as it were the very beginning of love" (p. 24).

Dating

Happy Marriage?

I am in my midtwenties and thinking about getting married. However, my friends and I are concerned that if we get married, our marriages will not be much different than the marriages of our parents and their friends. Is it really possible to have a happy marriage? How can I plan for a successful marriage?

Thank you for your thoughtful question. One of the most challenging issues about marriage is that people are either too negative about marriage or overly idealistic about marriage. Many have lost faith in the possibility of a good marriage, giving up altogether on marriage as a viable option. Others run blindly into marriage with a Pollyanna attitude, thinking that because they love each other so much, what has happened to others will not happen to them. Both positions are problematic.

It is important to realize, especially from a biblical perspective, that God instituted marriage. We should also remember that what God created was very good and was fashioned with our needs in mind. Therefore, marriage is a great idea with great possibilities, in spite of our sinful and imperfect condition.

On the other hand, because no one is perfect, no marriage is perfect either. Therefore, thinking that the trouble you have seen in other marriages will not happen to yours because you love each other is not realistic. The best of marriages experience trouble from time to time. Ask honest people who have been married for several decades and they will tell you that while their marriage may be stable and healthy, there are unresolved issues in their relationship that they are still working on.

Our response, then, is that the real answer to a successful marriage lies between the two opposite positions posed in your question. Marriage is wonderful. And yet, it is important to go into marriage with one's eyes wide open, being aware of the reality that every marriage, by definition, will experience bumpy times. Indeed, if you go into marriage knowing that it will not be perfect and that there are several stages each marriage will go through, you can expect problems, knowing that they are a part of the scenery on the journey of every marriage.

According to Michele Weiner-Davis, a prominent contemporary marriage researcher, the following are the five stages most marriages should expect to go through:

Passion Prevails: At this stage, couples concentrate on what they have in common, and they are dominated by an intense physical desire for each other. It is at this stage that many couples decide to marry. Survival tip: This stage will not last forever. However, when your ecstasy begins to fade, it doesn't mean your marriage is dying. This is a common cycle.

What Was I Thinking? After the honeymoon period of euphoria, couples have to get back to the mundane things of life, such as working and paying bills. During this time each person notices that the other isn't all they expected. Their spouse has bad breath in the morning and at other times; they spend too much time in the bathroom and don't clean up promptly after meals. The feelings of being in a fantasy world—which is what takes place in stage one—are now gone, and the couple is at the place where they need to make decisions about the rest of their lives.

For those in second marriages, the harsh reality of coordinating a blended family sets in. During this stage, couples question their sanity at the time they decided to marry the person they now seem to be stuck with for life. Survival tip: Be mindful of the fact that every marriage will experience conflict and challenges; then you will be better prepared to accept what is happening to you. Stay connected by spending time together in different activities and by making a vigorous sex life a high priority.

Everything Would Be Great if You Changed: The next several years are commonly taken up by couples trying to change their spouse. When the preferred change doesn't take place, couples often face a fork in the road, and some choose to divorce or to have affairs. Others decide to stick it out because of religious beliefs, financial considerations, or concern for their children. Among those who stay, some resign themselves to living in unhappy marriages, while others begin looking for better ways to communicate and manage conflict.

Couples who choose the latter option are the ones who are blessed, because the best of marriage is yet to come. Survival tip: Keep in mind that every marriage has stormy periods. Engaging the help of a professional

Christian counselor may be a good thing at this time. Research suggests that 86 percent of unhappy couples that stay together despite the conflict say that they are much happier five years later.

That's Just the Way He/She Is: This is the stage at which couples accept the fact that they will never be on the same page about everything with their spouse, so they seek ways to live in peace amid the differences. Spouses realize at this stage that learning to forgive is important if they are going to make it. Some mature to the point where they recognize that marriage is like everything else in life: there is always some bad with the good, and one needs to emphasize the positive. Survival tip: Don't ever make the mistake of thinking that you have "arrived" in your relationship. Continue to nurture your relationship every day by spending time together, talking, and touching.

Together at Last: By the time couples get to this stage of their marriage they have spent quite a bit of time together making history. They have come to the place where they agree that marriage is difficult and have a sense of accomplishment because of the trials they have faced together and have overcome. They have a greater appreciation for the strengths of their spouse and are no longer as easily threatened by their differences. Because their children are now older and more independent, this gives couples more time to focus on each other and enjoy more quality time together.

There is a sense that they have come full circle and have learned the dance of marriage. Survival tip: Keep yourself healthy and active so that you can enjoy the fruits of your labor. Remember that marriage is worth fighting for each and every day.

We believe that if you are mindful of what we have shared above, you and your friends have the capacity to have a happy and meaningful marital relationship. You may do well also to remember that with God all things are possible (Luke 18:27).

Don't Miss the Red Flag

I am a sophomore in college and have been in a relationship with my boyfriend for almost a year. He is a Christian who loves the Lord and is studying to be a physician. He is very intelligent and studies hard and has motivated me to excel in my classes. Recently, he pushed me while we were arguing about something, and I started to cry. He promised to never do it again, but now I'm frightened. How do I know if I'm in an abusive relationship?

We applaud you for recognizing something is not right in your relationship. Our feeling is your boyfriend has probably pushed you before and it has taken you awhile to seek help and counsel regarding this situation.

Abuse in relationships is a very difficult topic for anyone to speak about, especially for young men. So if you are reading this and are male and experiencing a similar situation, this is also for you. The truth is that everyone needs to get involved in better understanding abuse and knowing what resources are available to support those who need them.

As nice as your boyfriend may seem, he may have some issues about dealing with anger. This is not something you can help him with or change for him; he needs professional help. It is easy to be fooled when a person has many of the traits you are looking for in a potential mate. While he may be a Christian and very studious, it is possible his temper may be under the control of Satan. We know God can heal and forgive anything, and He can certainly heal and forgive your boyfriend. However, while your boyfriend is healing, should he choose to get help, you may get hurt more than you already have been.

Here are some sobering facts about abuse among young adults in relationships:

- Women ages twenty to twenty-four are at the greatest risk of nonfatal intimate partner violence.
- According to the Oregon Law Center, one in five teens in a serious relationship reports having been hit, slapped, or pushed by a partner.
- Fourteen percent of teens report their boyfriend or girlfriend threatened to harm them or themselves to avoid a breakup.
- Several studies indicate that as a dating relationship becomes more serious the potential for and nature of violent behavior also escalates.

- Date rape accounts for almost 70 percent of sexual assaults reported by adolescent and college-age women; 38 percent of those women are between fourteen and seventeen years old.

While being in a close relationship with another person is a deep desire God created us with, relationships are very complicated. This means you need to be smart about whom to date and how you date. The way you are treated by the person you are dating is probably a snapshot of the way that person will treat you when you are married. Healthy relationships follow the principles of 1 Corinthians 13:4–8: patience, kindness, self-control, and many other virtues. True love will not hurt you.

We recommend that you seriously think about terminating this relationship; however, we know you will ultimately have to make this decision for yourself. We just hope you do it before it is too late. If you are in college, get help from the school counselor. You may also get help from your pastor or campus chaplain. You should also tell your parents about this situation so they can give you the needed support and guidance.

God is the source of all love. He loves you more than you could ever ask, think, or imagine. So we hope that from this day forward you will trust your relationships to God and your quest for finding the right future spouse for yourself.

Wrong Love, Right Move

I recently ended a ten-month relationship with a man who was verbally abusive to me. He is very jealous and intimidated by me. I have a profession and a good job; I make good money and own my own home. What's wrong with that? I figure that's why he talks to me so badly. I always hear statements such as, "You independent women think you don't need a man; someday you will." Or he'll make chauvinistic remarks. He also likes to juggle two and three women at a time. I found out about one of them and confronted him about it. Of course, he denied it and told me it was my imagination and that I was assuming things. I found out about all of this last week and ended the relationship. It hurt me so badly to end it, because I knew I would miss his calling me, e-mailing me, and taking me out. There were some good times, but the bad outweighed the good. My question is, Why do I miss him so much? I didn't enjoy being talked to the way he talked to me. It made me feel horrible. Most of the time we were together or on the phone, it would end in an argument, and I would feel frustrated and stressed out. I felt betrayed when I found out about the other woman. Why does it bother me to see him with someone else? I should be glad I'm free from him, right? Can you give me some advice on how to shake these feelings, besides praying about it?

We are sorry to hear about your relationship going sour. Your story is not unique from many others that we have heard. Terminating your relationship with a man who seemed insecure about your financial stability and security, however, was the right thing to do. It is possible that running around with other women and being verbally abusive were actions that helped your former friend feel less insecure and in control in the relationship. People who feel inadequate in certain situations often put down others to make themselves feel better. Of course, such behavior is neither appropriate nor helpful.

The fact that you miss your friend is also not strange. He gave you attention that fed you emotionally. And now that the attention has stopped there is a vacuum where the interest once was. It is worthy of note that emotional connection is not a zero-sum game—all or nothing. There was a part of you that disliked what he said and did to you, and another part of you enjoyed his company and attention.

We often share that the best predictor of what a person will be like after marriage is what they are like before marriage. This is obviously not the type of relationship you want to be involved with. Move on. You made the right choice. While it is true that there is no perfect relationship, the preference is to be in a relationship that is happy with some sad times, rather than a relationship that is sad with some happy times.

As you already know, you will be missing this man until you have rid yourself of your emotional connection to him. If you have access to a good Christian counselor, attending a few sessions to work out your feelings is a great idea. Unless you take the time to get over this relationship in an intentional and deliberate way, you will cheat your next relationship of the real and genuine joy it has the potential to bring.

God has promised to supply all your needs. Trust Him for your next steps. And remember, it is better to be alone than to be in bad company.

We hope you will experience the peace of God that passes all understanding. We are praying for you.

Look Before You Leap

Recently I started dating a widowed father at my church who has been interested in me ever since I moved here. We've been hanging out with each other trying to get to know each other better during the past three weeks. I'm really enjoying the time we are spending together. He is extremely thoughtful and helpful. I even found out last night that he has been reading the book The 5 Love Languages. *It made so much sense because he has been speaking my primary love language for some time, and I'm discovering other ones that are stronger for me than I originally thought. I'd really like to get your opinion and advice. This is all very new to me, especially since he has three children. I just want to be careful not to hurt his children.*

T hank you for your thoughtful question. You are really the only one who can decide if this is a good fit for you. We are assuming this man and you share the same faith. If you do not, it isn't a good idea, since much of the empirical research suggests the risks are too great. If you share the same faith, and he is a widower, you should have no difficulty finding biblical grounds for marriage.

When one becomes involved with someone who has been married and has children, one needs to be aware of certain realities and determine whether one can live with them. You would want to consider the following:

His deceased wife will always be a part of his life and conversation with his children. And her relatives will always be related to his children and to him.

These children may sooner or later decide they do not like you, and may be hoping you have no ideas about replacing their mother. Currently you are not married to their father, and you are still experiencing the literal intoxication that new romantic relationships bring. So, for the moment, these children appear to be very nice and well behaved, but that can easily change.

If you marry this man and move into his home, you may bring habits to the family unlike his first wife, which he or the children may object to. Your special recipe for a particular dish will almost certainly be compared to the deceased wife's (and mom's) culinary skills, and probably unfairly.

Our advice is that you go into this relationship with your eyes wide open. True love may decide to overlook certain flaws, but it is certainly not blind; that is infatuation. Since you appear to be pretty interested in this man, we suggest rigorous premarital counseling before you decide to get married, or even before you have a wedding date in mind.

The pastor or counselor providing your premarital process should be certified to do this kind of work, and should be able to provide you with diagnostic inventories that are able to identify the strengths and growth areas in your relationship. This process will offer you the opportunity to find out how good your chances are to make this relationship work.

Please keep in mind that any relationship has the potential for disaster. The more complexity there is in a relationship, the more issues you will be dealing with. Therefore, do not be idealistic. Remember, there are no perfect relationships because there are no perfect people. Do not ignore red flags, and deal with them to your satisfaction. Do not be afraid, but be wise, and pray for God's guidance and leadership; then, listen and obey.

We hope you will take every step with your hand in God's. We are praying for you.

Controlling a Temper

My girlfriend and I have been dating for several months and recently started premarital counseling. What I am a little worried about is her bad temper and controlling attitude. When we are with the counselor she agrees to do what the counselor assigns for homework. However, she gets angry about the issues I have raised in the session and does not follow up with the assignment. I think she is just going through a phase and will act right once we get married. What do you think?

Congratulations on the premarital counseling. What you are doing is a very smart thing. It is like studying for a college physics exam, rather than just winging it based on what you think you logically know about the subject. It is like using a global positioning system to drive to an unknown destination in an unfamiliar city, rather than hoping you will get lucky and find the right place.

Being in love is an awesome experience, particularly when the person you feel special about loves you back. The longer you remain in a relationship, though, the trickier it becomes. Since God made us sociable beings, it feels good to have someone to hang out with when you feel like going out to the mall to shop, out to eat, out to a concert, or just staying at home to chill. The challenge is that we tend to get used to the person without critically thinking about whether our personalities mesh, or whether we have similar goals in life. As time goes by there is a greater likelihood that the real person will show up.

Now, we all have strengths and growth areas in our lives. However, if your special person has character flaws that he or she refuses to grow out of, you will need to decide if the defect is one you can tolerate or one you simply cannot live with. The tendency is to ignore the bad behavior and think that he or she will change when you finally get married and live together. This is no time to play games. Be honest with yourself. If your girlfriend is behaving badly before you get married, she will behave much worse after you say, "I do."

Pray earnestly to God to give you clarity of mind and courage to make decisions that will place your future on a solid foundation.

Making Decisions

Your column has been a blessing to me and my friends; thank you for your excellent work. I am going to be thirty-two years old this summer. I am dating a young lady and the relationship is now in trouble, and it is all on me. My life's dream was to be married by age twenty-five, and I have missed that deadline, but that's fine. I have only had two girlfriends in the past ten years. The problem is that I need some serious, God-inspired, personal counseling from experts such as you. I don't believe in divorce, but I know I can't last in a marriage that I am not happy with. My girlfriend is waiting for me to pop the question and so is the whole world. This is the second time we've been dating. I broke up with her the first time a year and a half ago. I ended up pursuing her again after I moved to where I currently live. I don't have the guts to break her heart twice, especially after I pursued her both times, but now we are heading that way again. After praying about it, and then getting back with her last fall, I was very excited and thought I was going to get married, for sure. I am tired of these back and forth feelings. I am not happy and need counsel on this and on my future. I don't feel that I can break it off, but I feel that if we get married it will be a countdown to a divorce or serious marital issues. As a Christian, I don't want to be that husband. If we do break up, I need advice on finding and getting along with the right person. I have been asking for advice from God on this one, and now I don't feel that I can be in the relationship any longer. I am asking God to help the next one to be the right one, but I am scared that I can end up feeling the same way. I desperately want to get married, but I want a happy and blessed union. Please help me ASAP.

It is important for you to know that marriage solves no problems; it only makes the existing ones worse. If you have a nagging feeling about your current relationship and cannot come to terms with it, there is no reason to pursue that association any longer. The quicker you come to terms with your true feelings and desires for this relationship, the better it will be for both of you. Your ambivalence is neither good for you nor for your girlfriend. The Christian thing to do is to confront your true point of view on where you see the relationship going. If you cannot see yourself with this young woman and this is the second time you are trying to convince yourself of the possibility of the relationship, you need to quit wasting this young woman's time. Time is what life is made up of, and when you waste someone's time, you waste their life.

On the other hand, if you believe that you simply cannot make up your mind when you have to deal with difficult and important decisions, you may do well to sign up for a few sessions with a reputable Christian counselor to make sure you are not the one with the problem. At any rate, you need to be honest with yourself, with the person you are seeing, and with God. Do not play games with yourself. If today you are convinced that there are issues in the relationship that you simply cannot live with, walk away before you destroy someone else's life as well as your own. Do not do what many others have done in the past to the detriment of their lives. They believe that the person they are hoping to marry will somehow change, and that the issues they are disturbed about today will somehow vanish magically. While nothing is impossible, this situation is not a plausible one.

Again, we encourage you to see a reputable Christian counselor and take care of your own emotional health before pursuing a new relationship. We hope you will enjoy God's greatest gift in the person of Jesus Christ, and trust Him to lead you to the life He has already planned for you.

The Advantages and Disadvantages of Shacking Up

Isn't living together before marriage a good way to discover problems in a relationship and learn how to handle them in the future?

Widespread among young adults today is the notion that living together before marriage is a good way to find out if you can get along with a potential marriage partner, thus avoiding a bad marriage. The available research on the effects of cohabitation, however, does not confirm this belief. Much of the investigation on this topic has shown quite a lot of evidence to the contrary. To be sure, those who live together before marriage are more likely to experience a broken relationship than those who do not.

According to *The State of Our Unions, 2012,* studies suggest that between 1960 to 2011 the number of unmarried couples in America increased more than seventeen times. Estimates based on recent research proffer that about 25 percent of unmarried women between the ages of twenty-five to thirty-nine are currently living with a partner, in addition to 25 percent who lived with a partner at some time in the past. To be sure, more than 60 percent of first-time marriages are now preceded by living together, compared to virtually none fifty years ago. Despite this reality, the divorce rate has not really decreased, and there are many other negative consequences to this kind of arrangement.

Worthy of note—according to much of the current research—is that cohabitation is more likely to take place among people who are less religious than their peers, those who have experienced divorce, those whose parents have divorced, those whose fathers have been absent from their lives, or those who have experienced their parents' high level of marital distress during childhood.

For us, more important than all of the research findings, are God's directives about how we should live our lives. From the beginning of time God ordained that it was not good for man to be alone (Genesis 2:18) and made Eve out of the side of Adam and blessed the first couple (marriage). In the New Testament, the apostle Paul is inspired by God to share that "because of sexual immorality, let each man have his own wife, and let each woman have her own husband" (1 Corinthians 7:2).

Of course, the postmodern perspective is to question everything, especially that which gives counsel to one's personal life and moral behavior. Nevertheless, any way you slice this issue—from a spiritual or secular perspective—the answer is pretty much the same: couples who live together before marriage experience higher levels of marital distress and divorce than their peers who did not.

Trust God in your personal intimate life and realize that His plan is always the best. Trust Him, and you will be led to the right relationship and given the power to live victoriously for Christ.

What Should I Do?

I am a divorced Christian woman who has been through a horrendous marriage filled with neglect, verbal and physical abuse, financial struggles, adultery (on his part), and depression. Until very late last year I loathed the male population and figured there were no decent, respectable men still on the face of this earth. Then after much prayer, studying, counseling, more prayer, and fasting, God healed my wounds and allowed me to realize that I had unreasonably and unrealistically put all men in the category of worthless. Well, to make the story short, I woke up one day realizing I truly wanted to enjoy the experience of being loved and sharing my love and life with someone.

I began to pray daily for God's direction in this matter and for very specific characteristics I truly desired in that special man. After praying daily for nearly three months, I met a very special man who I realized, after a good many conversations as well as time together over several months, possesses these strengths. So now the problem is that I care very deeply for him but I know he is reluctant to have any further relationship due to his own experiences. I don't wish to compromise a beautiful relationship by causing any undue pressure. I am not seeking to run down any aisle but also don't want to walk away from what I, in my heart and through much prayer, feel the Lord delivered into my hands. Do I share my feelings with him at this point or wait to allow things to possibly develop later on? If I tell him, recognizing that he is not ready to hear such, I run the risk of chasing him off. If I don't tell him and just continue as is, am I waiting for the "pie in the sky" that may never appear? Yes, we are very compatible and share a very special bond even from the start. I don't feel any desire whatsoever to see anyone else, and no, he is not the first or last person to have asked me out. What do you think?

We are sorry to hear about the pain you have been through in your previous relationship and are pleased to know that the Lord has healed you in a remarkable way.

Now about your new situation, we want to caution you by stating that being attracted to someone is not reason enough to believe that "this is the one," even if the person has several of the traits you have prayed for in a mate. At the beginning of a relationship most people appear to be compatible because they speak only about things they have in common. There are other more important indicators, however, that need to be evident at this time. For example, in an honest relationship—when a person you are seeing is not playing games with you—it is perfectly fine to get a progress report on the relationship. If you have spent time together over several months—according to your account—there is obviously an interest on both your parts. In your own words, you already "care very deeply for him." Apparently, the time you have spent together has generated within you strong feelings for this man. However, if this man has not, for whatever reason, also begun to care deeply about you, it is important for you to find out immediately and deal with the reality of the situation.

When a man asks you out, he is usually interested in you, or at the very least fascinated with being in your company. If the same man continues to see you for several months, he is clearly receiving a certain degree of satisfaction from the relationship. Whatever social or emotional benefits this man has obtained from you in the time you have spent together during several months of friendship is a privilege he has enjoyed. It is very important for you to keep in mind that for every privilege we have in life there is a corresponding responsibility. The privilege of enjoying any relationship has a matching responsibility of commitment. For this reason alone you have the right to ask him what he is looking for in the relationship. If that frightens him away, he is not the one

On the other hand, sometimes men are afraid of making a deeper commitment to a relationship because they lack the financial stability to pursue the relationship to the next level. It is also possible for men or women to have been deeply hurt by a previous relationship and they may be fearful of seriously committing themselves to being hurt again. If either one of these is the situation in this case you should still be able to talk about that reality honestly in order to be able to assess whether the relationship has the potential of becoming a serious and lasting relationship or not.

Again, we would encourage you not to play games with your emotions. You should not be afraid to lose a relationship with anyone because you need to ask honest and necessary questions. If you are very compatible with a particular person and you are meant for each other, then you will also be honest with each other. If God has presumably sent this person to you, then you should have nothing to be afraid about. Remember, God has a thousand different ways to supply your needs. If this man means business and cares for you he will welcome the opportunity to share with you his hopes and dreams. If he is just a player, or has other unresolved issues that keep him from further pursuing a committed relationship with you, you should be glad to see him disappear.

Trust God to help you decide not only with your heart but also with your head. If God has sent this man to you as a possible life partner, He will also give you the courage to speak without fear. Any man who runs away when asked a serious question about his intentions in a relationship is not really serious about you. Continue to pray, and ask God to lead you to the relationship that will allow you to be at peace and maximize your talents for Jesus.

Attraction to Older Women

I enjoy reading your column in the Message *magazine. I never thought I'd actually be writing to you for advice. I am a twenty-five-year-old single man who has never been married or had any children. I am attracted to a woman in my church who happens to be fourteen years older than I am. This woman also has never been married nor does she have any children. We do have a lot in common. We are both college graduates and have professional jobs. In today's society, it is said that "age ain't nothing but a number." Since she and I are both mature adults, should either one of us be concerned about the age difference? Your advice will be appreciated.*

It would appear that pop culture is enamored with the older woman–younger man syndrome these days, and as things go in our postmodern era, life often imitates art. However, when it comes to matters of the heart (relationships), a Christian would want to base his or her decisions on much more than what is or appears to be popular.

To begin with, here are a few questions you would want to ask yourself before entering a relationship that will potentially lead to marriage: (1) Do you share a similar love for God and belief in the Bible? (2) Is she a kind, pleasant, and positive person? (3) Do you enjoy the same kinds of leisure activities? (4) Do you share similar goals for your lives? (5) Were you reared with similar values and want many of the same things in life? (6) How important to you is having biological children? (7) Has she been seriously involved in long-term relationships with other men? (8) Are your respective families supportive of your relationship? We believe that answering these questions honestly will give you a good idea about the chances that you have for success in your potential relationship.

As for the age difference, it can play a significant role in your relationship, but it doesn't necessarily have to. At twenty-five years of age you have just arrived at the point in your life where your center of judgment (found in the prefrontal cortex of the brain) has fully developed. If you were twenty years old and she were thirty-four, we would be more concerned. However, based on the profile you have shared of yourself and the woman who has caught your interest, you both seem to have a lot going for you. While women tend to mature earlier than men, if you are a mature twenty-five (not all twenty-five-year-olds are) and she is a mature thirty-nine (not all thirty-nine-year-olds are) and you are comfortable with each other's level of maturity, we do not see a big problem.

We would caution you about banking your relationship purely on attraction, though. Being attracted to someone is not necessarily a viable basis for a meaningful and solid relationship, especially if the attraction is merely physical. If you are attracted to beautiful inner qualities such as kindness, patience, gentleness, industriousness, spirituality, a strong work ethic, and commitment to loved ones, then your attraction is really significant. Also, if you find that you are mostly attracted to much older women you may want to explore that with a reputable Christian counselor. Your attraction to older women doesn't have to be a problem, especially if you are not attracted only to older women.

We encourage you to make the most of life every day, and from this day forward trust God to lead you in a path that will make you of greatest service to those around you.

Sharing My Name at Marriage

I'm getting married in a few months to a young woman who refuses to change her name until I understand the pain of losing my identity. She has really created a rift in our relationship—just a few months away from the wedding. I have tried to understand. I asked if she'd be willing to compromise by hyphenating her name, but she refused. I really think this is stupid. I feel that she is trying to be stubborn and difficult. My fiancée just feels like going contrary to tradition. I'm having second thoughts about even getting married to her. I see us in a catch-22. Thanks for your time.

We are very sorry to hear that your girlfriend's refusal to give up her name at marriage is causing you so much pain. Of course, such a position is not unusual these days, and there is nothing biblical or ethical that we know about that you can use to convince her otherwise. Indeed, there are some places in North America, right now, where women are not even allowed to take their husband's name at marriage.

Our suggestion is that you "seek first to understand, then to be understood." Whatever the situation, allow yourself to be open-minded, and truly try to understand where your girlfriend is coming from. You don't need to agree with her—just try to understand where she is coming from. If you genuinely allow yourself to go through this process, we guarantee you that the environment will be totally different for both of you. Once you understand where she is coming from, being as objective as you can possibly be, calmly and patiently share your position with your girlfriend.

If nothing changes with either one of you after praying for humility and understanding, and communicating on this matter in a nonthreatening environment and in a nonthreatening manner, you need to come to grips with the situation and make a decision. Be honest with yourself. Don't play any games. Only you know what you can and can't live with. However, ask yourself if your decision is based on spiritual values or simply on your need to be "the man."

I want you to know that as a man (this is Willie's comment) I clearly empathize with your position and know that twenty years ago I would have felt the same way. However, today, after twenty years of marriage to a woman who couldn't have come to me any other way but as a gift from God, I ask myself the question: Would I have married her if her position had been like that of your girlfriend? I shudder to think that I may have given up such a significantly blessed experience because of a decision based on a patriarchal tradition of viewing women—consciously or unconsciously—as personal property.

If you really love this woman, and so far you have not identified significant issues of religious values and/or practices in your premarital counseling that would impede you from proceeding with the wedding, we would counsel you not to "cut off your nose to spite your face." After all, a few years from now your girlfriend (wife then) may have grown comfortable with the notion of taking your name. However, this is your life, and only you can make this decision. If the Lord has led you so far, trust Him to lead you some more. We will be praying for you.

Facing the Fork in the Road

I'm seventy-six years old and a widow. About five years after my husband died, I started seeing a gentleman from my church who is about my age and whom I like very much. We have talked about marriage several times, and I would like to be married to him, but he takes care of a mentally disabled son who is in his forties and who dislikes me a lot. I've encouraged my friend to put his son in a nursing home, but he refuses to do so. I want to get married to this gentleman, but I cannot and will not live with his son. What do you suggest?

Your question is very complex and has several layers. However, we will try to give it our best shot, based on the limited information we have about the situation.

First, we are delighted for you that after the pain and grief of losing a spouse you have found love again. Second, you are very blessed to have found someone for the second time whom you care about and who cares about you enough to consider marriage. Third, you have clearly come to a fork in your relationship road and need to make a decision rather soon or risk losing your peace of mind.

From our vantage point, you have several options. However, they boil down to making your peace with the idea of living in the same house with a person who will become your stepson, or walking away from a relationship with the man you love.

The fact that your friend refuses to put his son in a nursing home says a lot about his character and commitment to relationships with people he loves. Apparently, he believes that he is still in a position to care for the needs of his son, and would prefer to continue doing so rather than leaving him in the care of others. This is commendable and speaks to the commitment this man may demonstrate for you should you need similar care.

Your objection to living with a mentally impaired son who dislikes you is not a terminal condition. It is very possible that the son is afraid of losing the attention he currently receives from his father if you come into the picture permanently. You can change the son's perceptions and feelings toward you by the way you treat the son when you visit the home of your friend. If you are attentive and kind to the son rather than wanting all the attention of his father for yourself, it is very possible that the negative treatment you are currently experiencing from the son may change to more pleasant exchanges.

Of course, the other choice is to simply walk away from the relationship and to look for one who is more to your liking. You already know that there are no guarantees.

Remember, "all things work together for good to them who love God" (Romans 8:28). In your situation it is possible that God is trying to mold your character in a certain direction to make you of greater use to Him. Take advantage of this opportunity, rather than walk away from the blessings God may have sent your way.

We hope you will earnestly seek God in prayer and ask Him to guide you in the way He wants you to go. May you find peace with the decision God leads you to make.

Is Premarital Counseling Necessary?

My boyfriend of three years and I are thinking about getting married. Someone at church said I should think about getting premarital counseling. Is that really necessary? How will premarital counseling help us? We already have many wedding-related expenses; why spend more than we need to?

Congratulations on your wedding plans. Marriage is a good thing. And it is especially great when you are thinking about marrying someone you have known for several years. Sharing the same faith and values are essential, since our values grow out of our core beliefs about God and the universe.

We will admit that we do have a bias in favor of premarital counseling, or premarital preparation/education, as we prefer to refer to this type of activity.

Here is why: (1) When people are dating they often try to justify their decision to be with that person and often look only for the things they have in common, rather than the differences that exist. (2) There is a tendency to be romantic, foster feelings of warmth, spend time hugging, kissing, and unfortunately sometimes more than that—allowing one's heart to dictate the pace of the relationship, rather than talking through important issues. (3) People often assume an "If loving you is wrong, I don't wanna be right" attitude, overlooking red flags, ignoring the objective counsel of others.

It is important to know a person before you marry him. Good premarital education allows you to talk about things you don't ordinarily talk about, such as each other's family background—whether you were raised by two parents or a single parent, or if your parents or your fiancé's parents were divorced, and so on. All this information is important, because it speaks to your expectations about marriage, and to what kind of baggage you are bringing to the relationship. And this is just one of the things you will discuss, to say nothing of religious persuasion and practice, children, finances, sexual history and expectations, fostering good communication, and so on.

Will premarital counseling help you? As long as there are two flawed—that's all of us—human beings in a relationship there will be problems. Expect them. However, being acquainted with problem-solving techniques and having Christian values that lead you to trust God for help when you have done your best, are keys to giving your marriage a fighting chance. If you think premarital preparation is expensive, believe us when we say that the alternative is much more expensive.

Dating Around. Does It Really Work?

My parents tell me to date around, get to know different people before settling down. But when I do, guy friends call me a player and the girls think I'm a dog. Is there a way to date around and not mislead people?

We believe that dating around is definitely not the way to a lasting and committed relationship. As you can see, it has led you to your present dilemma, and it sounds as though you want out.

Dating around implies playing a game of spin the bottle, if you will, till we get to the right one. Dating is real if it occurs with real people who have real feelings; it's not an opportunity to "play" at relationships.

Dating around is intimacy without commitment, intimacy being when two people journey into the secret places of each other's lives. Once you begin this journey, it is a natural progression that two healthy people spending lots of time alone together will develop a physical affection toward one another. It's perfectly normal. God made us to be sexual beings who feel sexual desire for people we care for.

Although we can choose not to act on these feelings, it often becomes the natural next step in the dating process. How many times and with how many people can you do this without ruining your ability for true intimacy when you are ready to "settle down"?

If you are truly interested in getting to know people, we suggest you develop friendships. Friendship focuses on a common interest shared by two (or more) people. The focus is not your relationship but the common interest you share. Friendship is the best foundation on which to build a lasting committed relationship. At some point, you may realize that one of your friends may be a potential mate, and you may pursue a dating relationship—that is very different from "dating around."

We want to encourage you to reevaluate your attitude and values about dating. Concentrate on what God's will is for your life. Allow God to transform your thinking about dating, which will most likely directly oppose the secular world's thinking on the subject. In Philippians 1:9, the apostle Paul writes, "So this is my prayer: that your love will flourish and that you will not only love much but well. Learn to love appropriately. You need to use your head and test your feelings so that your love is sincere and intelligent, not sentimental gush" (*The Message*).

We wish you the best.

Defining Fornication

What does fornication involve? I know that fornication is sex before marriage, but when it comes to dating, is kissing and touching an act of fornication as well?

*V*ine's Expository Dictionary of Biblical Words *states that* fornication *is derived from the Greek word* porneia, *from which we get the term* *pornography*. The word is used throughout the Old and New Testaments and stands for inappropriate sexual activity, which includes adultery, and commonly refers to "sex for hire" or "sex for kicks."

If your purpose is to find a simple and technical answer to the question you posed, then, based on this definition, "kissing and touching" would not be considered fornication. Understand, of course, that dating is a foreign notion to Bible times. Furthermore, the essence of your question is complex and demands much more than a simple yes or no, or yet just another definition of the word fornication. When it comes to questions like these, every Christian needs to develop personal responsibility based on a process of spiritual development (praying earnestly, ability to self-criticize, and openness to the Spirit).

So let's dig beneath the surface of your original question. You asked about "kissing and touching," which is also known as petting. Petting, roughly defined, starts anywhere after an affectionate hug and ends before intercourse. It involves the touching of one another's sexually excitable areas. Sometimes young people engage in petting just because they think it is expected of them. Sometimes petting happens out of habit or boredom. For some, petting satisfies their need for affection and self-esteem. For most, petting satisfies their basic human need for intimacy—a desire to be close to someone else, to be known deeply and to know someone else deeply, to be loved and to love, to feel significant. The Creator created us all with this desire for intimacy.

However, while petting does provide a certain level of intimacy, it too often becomes a substitute for true intimacy and catapults you too quickly to a very high level of physical intimacy. If you want your relationship to reach its full potential, it must move systematically through certain stages, stages that lead to a level of emotional vulnerability—such as friendship, the sharing of private thoughts and feelings. Couples who engage in petting very early in a relationship short-circuit this process and fall into the rut of gaining intimacy primarily through sexual activity, and they never really get to know each other. What starts as mere kissing then has to progress to a deeper level to achieve the closeness that both parties want. Even if the petting doesn't progress to intercourse, at this point you have handed over very intimate parts of yourself to someone who may not be appropriate or worthy of your sexuality or intimacy. Most adolescents and young adults (and even more mature adults) forget that intercourse is not the only sexual act with serious consequences. The reality is that the more people you "kiss and touch," the more detrimental it is to your ability to be intimate when you are ready for a lifelong relationship.

First Corinthians 6:18–20 speaks about the painful impact of unwise sexual involvement in relationships. In these verses Paul also talks about our bodies being temples of God. So as Christians, everything that we do is somehow related to our relationship with Christ. Remember that God designed us as sexual beings. However, God designed us with something even more powerful—our brains. So just because we are sexual doesn't mean we have to give in to our hormones.

If you haven't done so already, develop a plan of action before you find yourself in an intimate situation. Determine what your boundaries will be; what will be off-limits when it comes to physical touch; what settings (alone in an apartment, car, isolated areas, dark rooms, and so on) are off-limits to be alone with the other person; what kinds of clothing will you wear, and so on. Ask yourself where "kissing and touching" fit into who you are as a person and the sort of person God expects you to be. Act as if you are writing your autobiography. How and where does petting fit into it?

This is just a brief response to your question and the beginning of your quest to "do the right thing," which ultimately should be what God wants you to do. We encourage you not just to seek easy answers in your Christian journey. Take every opportunity to develop spiritually. May God grant you wisdom and courage.

Dating After Separation

When is a good time to start dating after a marital separation?

Our answer assumes that by marital separation you mean divorce, since individuals who are not divorced—despite being separated—should not be dating other people. After all, if one is not divorced, one is still married. And if one is still married, it is not morally proper to be dating other people.

Now that we are clear about what we are answering, we suggest that it takes at least two to three years to work through the readjustments of divorce before one is ready to consider remarriage. The period of recovery following a divorce is approximately three to five years. You will find our response pretty consistent with what is recommended by many other family professionals.

There are several questions one should seriously ask before complicating one's life with a new relationship. Among the questions you should ask yourself are the following: (1) How did I relate to my past spouse? (2) What was positive and what was negative about the way we related to each other? (3) What have I learned about myself since my divorce? (4) How can I change the destructive patterns in my former relationship, which will inevitably arise in my next relationship unless I am intentional about identifying the behaviors and dealing with them? (5) Have I attempted to rebuild my life since my divorce and am I emotionally over my first marriage? (6) How much time should I give to my former spouse and his or her relatives since ongoing communication is necessary because of finances, children, business partnerships, and in-laws?

Such questions should be identified and dealt with properly, preferably through professional counseling, so that both your new spouse and you will know what to expect from your former relational ties, which may include biological children or stepchildren, for instance.

When it comes to intimate relationships, and this is true for a first marriage and especially a second marriage, a good rule of thumb is to move slowly and carefully. Above all else, seek God's guidance through prayer.

Sexual Relationships

Intermittent Intimacy

I have been married more than forty mostly happy years. In the last year, I have been turned away with a laugh, or simply ignored, when I suggest to my wife that we be intimate. I am at the place now where I almost never ask, because when I get that response I feel I'm not wanted. Now we engage in intimacies about once a week, mostly on the same day, and always first thing in the morning, when we have to hurry so we can get to work. There is really nothing to look forward to. I keep clean and well groomed, and have basically given myself to please my wife. I love her and don't want to trip up from desire. Any suggestions?

When it comes to intimacy between married couples, there are many reasons a spouse—especially a woman—may not be as willing or as comfortable to be intimate as often as in the past. By your own admission you seem to be having encounters with your spouse about once per week. We would say that after more than forty years of marriage, you are doing quite well. While it is true that a married couple may enjoy intimate fulfillment during their sixties, seventies, and even beyond, there are many changes that often take place with the aging process; frequency of intimacy is one of them.

We also must be mindful that on average, an adult human male body produces approximately seven to eight times more testosterone than an adult female body. Partly because of this biochemical difference, a man tends to think about and appears to be more interested in physical intimacy more often than his wife. This does not mean, however, that the wife has lost interest. The truth is, the closer couples feel in their relationship to each other, and the better their communication, the better their intimacy with each other will be.

Instead of feeling ignored and rebuffed, seriously consider having a nonthreatening conversation with your wife to let her know how you feel about the changes you perceive in your intimacy. Use "I" messages in your conversation with your wife, such as "I feel hurt and rejected when I approach you for intimacy and you ignore me or push me away. Is there something happening with you that you would like to share with me?" Then give your wife an opportunity to explain what is going on with her. Listen carefully to what she says, and try paraphrasing what you hear her say without being defensive or rebutting. The more your wife feels understood, the more quickly she will be interested in listening to your needs and trying to meet them.

We recommend that you read the book by Willard F. Harley Jr., titled *His Needs, Her Needs: Building an Affair-Proof Marriage.* You will find many eye opening realities as you read, and may even find how to make your situation better. You may also decide on a few sessions with a good Christian counselor.

Trust God to make you more understanding and keep you faithful until He comes. Nothing is worth missing out on heaven. You and your wife will continue in our prayers.

Sex No Longer a Priority

I am concerned about my diminishing desire for intimacy with my husband. I am fifty years old, and we have been married for many years. Recently I've found myself wanting to avoid sex often. Could this be related to menopause?

There are several reasons why women can lose interest in sexual relations in marriages. Just being fifty is not necessarily a reason for a diminished interest in sexual activity, although it may play a role. Menopause is a midlife transition for women between the ages of forty and sixty. It is the end of fertility, usually indicated by the permanent absence of monthly cycles. During this time the ovaries produce lower levels of the sex hormones estrogen and progesterone. Estrogen plays a significant role in the mental health of women. Lower levels of estrogen may lower the mood of a woman and contribute to other factors as well. This reality affects some women more than others, so checking with your physician is a good idea.

On the other hand, we believe a healthy marriage makes for a healthy sex life. Couples who feel good about each other tend to communicate well, do fun things together, like each other, make time for each other, and enjoy sexual activity on a regular basis regardless of age. By the same token, couples who are in a marriage filled with strife, constant disagreement and bickering, tend to have less desire to spend time together, and are less likely to enjoy a fulfilling sex life, even if they are much younger than you are.

The good news is that your present reality does not have to continue for the remainder of your life. We know, based on research and working with many couples, that husbands who understand the emotional needs of their respective wives, and are intentional about meeting those needs, have wives who return the favor. Every married couple should know that men and women are very different. Indeed, men and women are almost the exact opposite. While the primary need of women is to receive affection (don't confuse this with sex) and to have meaningful conversation with their own husbands, the primary need of men is to have sex with their respective wives. One does not happen without the other.

It means then, unless there is a physical or psychological barrier that is keeping you from being interested in sex anymore, your marriage relationship needs to be improved so that your deep desire for intimacy with your husband will return.

First John 4:18 declares, "There is no fear in love; but perfect love casts out fear, because fear involves torment. But he who fears has not been made perfect in love."

Trust God to lead you and your husband to intentionally develop a better marriage relationship so that your lives together will be a powerful testimony of God's plan for joy in marriage.

Teenage Questions About Sex

I'm hearing a lot of teens at my church say that oral sex is not sex. As the family ministries leader at my church, how do I go about having a discussion group on this topic, and what kind of counsel would you give me to give to our young people?

This is a very serious question that deserves a very delicate and careful response. First of all, to engage in a conversation about sexuality with teens at your church, you must make sure that their parents are aware of what will be discussed and have consented in writing for their children to participate—especially if the youth involved are not yet eighteen years of age. Second, you must make sure that the person leading the discussion group is someone trusted and respected by your congregation and is one who has been approved by your church board. However, we support you in your desire to encourage your congregation to engage in this conversation with your youth.

We are aware that many young people, especially Christian young people, believe that oral sex is not really sex, and is an activity they can participate in because it is not intercourse and they will still remain virgins. To be sure, according to a recent groundbreaking study by the Centers for Disease Control and Prevention, more than 50 percent of fifteen- to nineteen-year-olds in the United States are involved in this type of activity. Psychologists and mental health professionals, however, believe that this kind of behavior among teens demonstrates their lack of understanding about the connection between intimate sexual behavior and emotional health and are at risk for developing emotionally warped relationships as adults.

It is important for Christian parents to understand that they cannot afford to not talk with their youth about sexuality. Sexuality is a gift of God that can be enjoyed to the fullest only when we follow God's instructions. For this to happen, parents must come to grips with their own sexuality and develop a level of comfort with this topic for the sake of their children. The earlier children are taught about healthy sexuality by their parents, the better their chances for developing a healthy and God-directed approach to sexuality by the time they are teens.

In 1 Corinthians 7, the apostle Paul makes clear that God's plan for sexuality is in the context of marriage. Only in this relationship of mature commitment and devotion to another individual, according to God, can sexual relations of any kind be appropriately handled.

Trust God to lead you to take on difficult subjects with your church family. When we safeguard the youth of the church we also protect the future of the church.

Honeymoon Woes

I got married recently. To be honest, I was expecting a more vigorous sex life with my husband, given all the excitement of being newlyweds and the anticipation after an eighteen-month nonsexual courtship. I'm finding sex to be very hard work and don't seem to have much interest in it at all. I thought it would just come naturally. My single friends at church are sure we're having a great time and can't wait for me to share my experiences with them, which I am avoiding. My friends outside of church laugh at me and say, "You should have tasted the apple before buying it." We both came into the relationship with a previous history, but decided that we wanted to bring the relationship under God's control from the very start. Could it be that we are living with the consequences of our sins? Does it get better? I pray so.

We are very sorry to hear about your less-than-exciting sex life at the beginning of your marriage. Please know that your experience is not unique. While a healthy sex life is important to any thriving marriage relationship, especially a young one, sex is not the most important aspect of marriage.

Like anything else in marriage, the more you appreciate each other and take the time to nurture your relationship and get to know each other better, the more you will enjoy your marriage, including sexual intercourse and sexual intimacy in general.

Nothing comes naturally in marriage. If that is an expectation of yours, you will be disappointed. However, you can take care of that easily by changing your expectations. Based on what you shared, we believe that you are allowing the expectations of your friends to rate too highly in your relationship. To give your marriage a fighting chance, you are going to have to learn to develop a little more privacy for your marriage from your friends, or the unnecessary pressure from your friends—perceived or real—will destroy your marriage.

One key element of turning things around in your marriage is your willingness to implement an important habit in all successful relationships: "Seek first to understand, then to be understood." If you try to understand your husband, and communicate your desire to really understand where he is coming from, you will be surprised how things get turned around more quickly than you think.

We hope you were able to read our September/October 2003 column on low sex drive. In that piece we explored the often-unspoken low sex drive in a significant number of men. If you communicate to your husband that he is less than satisfactory in bed, you will wound his ego tremendously. This is a time to have a heart-to-heart conversation with your husband in an environment that does not involve blame. Perhaps you can both talk about your less-than-adequate sexual experience so far. Who knows, the situation may be medical. As a wife, you want to remember the "in sickness and in health" vows you took. It is also a good idea to participate in a marriage conference or marriage retreat in your area.

Below are a couple of books you may want to read together.

1. *Getting Your Sex Life Off to a Great Start: A Guide for Engaged and Newlywed Couples,* by Clifford and Joyce Penner (Nashville: Word Publishing, 1994).
2. *The Sex-Starved Marriage: A Couple's Guide to Boosting Their Marriage Libido,* by Michele Weiner Davis (New York: Simon and Schuster, 2003).

It is important for you to continue trusting in the Lord. Remember, if you are in Christ, you are new creatures. Do not allow Satan, "the accuser of the brethren," to fill you with guilt about your past life, and keep you from enjoying the married life God wants you to have today. Trust in God, who has promised to supply all your needs.

We shall continue to pray for you and your husband. Remember that the power of God and commitment are the elements that make marriages last and thrive.

Low Sex Drive?

My husband and I are in our midthirties and have been married for a little more than six years. What concerns me is my husband's low interest in sexual intimacy with me. When I try to get close to him, he tells me it has been a long day at work and he is very tired and needs to rest. My girlfriends often talk about the fact that their husbands never seem to get enough sexual intimacy, and all the relationship workshops we attend give me the impression that men usually show more interest in these types of things. We seem to be different from most, and I am becoming frustrated and suspicious. I would appreciate your point of view.

Thank you for asking such an important question. While not the most significant aspect of marriage, sexual intimacy is a positive and essential part of the close bond developed by two human beings in marriage.

Sexual intimacy thrives in relationships in which couples openly share their feelings in an environment of trust, respect, and intimacy. For open communication to work effectively, however, there needs to be a balance of power between husband and wife. In marriage, couples often use communication techniques to manipulate their partner and always get what they want. In order for communication techniques to truly work, there must be an environment of trust. You need to know that your partner always has your best interests in mind.

Contrary to popular opinion, men are not the sex machines that our culture makes them out to be. While it is true that normally men tend to have higher rates of sexual desire because of much higher doses of testosterone in them than in women, this is not so for every man. In fact, "some studies suggest that as high as 50 percent of women and 20 percent of men say their sex drive isn't what it used to be."

The idea that women have low sexual desire is very common in our culture. Not so for men. In fact, to be a real man in Western culture is equal to having a great sexual appetite and being ready to perform sexually at the drop of a hat. It is a matter of male identity—that of being strong, in control, and always ready to perform.

We believe that situations such as the one you outlined above can be dealt with only in a very supportive environment of trust, respect, and deep concern for the other individual. Having a medical checkup and asking your primary-care physician for a professional opinion on the dilemma is very important. Many who have been through similar situations have found helpful advice from their physicians and/or have received a medical prescription to help alleviate the dilemma.

Since your husband has indicated being tired, perhaps planning a weekend getaway together to an enjoyable place where he can relax is something you might try after talking with his physician. If you cannot afford a weekend away, have relatives or friends baby-sit your children while you try to spend a low-key weekend together. Reminiscing about earlier days when life was simpler and easier is often what you need to get you back on track.

If the physician's visit and relaxing weekend do not improve your sexual relationship, it is essential for you to communicate with your husband in a caring and nondemanding way about how important it is for you to have frequent sexual encounters with him. Please do not gauge frequency of sexual intercourse by some national poll you have read about in a magazine or by what your girlfriends may be saying at work or at church. Appropriate frequency is anything that a couple agrees on and that is satisfying to their relationship. On the other hand, no one who is married can afford to disregard the feelings of a spouse who is sexually unhappy.

Trust in God to give you wisdom, patience, and grace to deal with this matter in the most supportive and respectful way possible.

Fun Sex?

My fiancé believes that sex is for procreation, not pleasure. That doesn't sound right, does it?

While it is true that sex is for propagation or procreation, the Bible clearly leads us to believe that sex is also intended for enjoyment. The biblical directive on sex is that it is to take place within marriage; it is an act of marriage. Many people believe that because the Bible speaks out forcefully against the abuse or misuse of sex, fornication, or adultery, then God must condemn all sex. The Bible condemns extramarital and premarital sex, but always speaks approvingly of sex within marriage.

Unfortunately, many Christians convince themselves that if something is spiritually acceptable to God it cannot be enjoyable. This belief leads many to deduce that if sex is enjoyed, it must be sinful. On the contrary, God created sex for procreation—"be fruitful and multiply"

(Genesis 1:22)—and definitely for our enjoyment. God designed us with immense artistry and care, ensuring that the male and female complement each other. We hasten to say that we are not talking about the perverted, abusive, and self-serving sex bandied about on television and in magazines and other media. We are talking about the pure, God-given mutual expression of love.

The book of Proverbs is filled with scriptural passages that signify the love-making experience as one that is not solely for propagation, but clearly intended for ecstatic pleasure (Proverbs 5:18, 19). Furthermore, it is undeniable in Song of Songs that the lovers are expressing passionate, unadulterated, and unashamed sexual passion for each other. It is dignified and egalitarian; there is genuine concern for the other's needs and pleasure.

The New Testament also gives us insight on sexual passion. In 1 Corinthians 7, Paul speaks about the sexual needs and drive that should be fulfilled in marriage and clearly shows that God fully understands the nature of the sexual drive—"it is better to marry than to burn with passion" (verse 9). To be sure, sex should not be used as a substitute for intimacy; rather, it is the most profound expression of love and intimacy. God's intent for sexual intimacy is relational. It helps us achieve the compelling oneness He designed for marriage.

We encourage you and your fiancé to explore—with guidance from your premarital counselor and/or your pastor—both of your attitudes, opinions, and beliefs about sex. Discuss how previously held notions or attitudes about sex may have contributed to your fiancé's arriving at the conclusion that sex is for procreation only. If you are planning to enter into marriage with this person, it is worth spending the time now to discuss this topic. Ask God to help you have patience, humility, and understanding that are needed as you explore this very delicate issue.

Infidelity

Lying Lips: An Abomination

While dating a wonderful woman, I casually started talking to another person, but never went on a date with her. Recently I texted my casual friend to see if she had feelings about us, and she said we could be only friends. My wonderful girlfriend found out about my text to the casual friend and confronted me. I denied it and told her that the other lady was the one who sent me the text. However, a mutual friend later informed me that she saw my text with her own eyes. My girlfriend then broke up with me. I apologized, and she said she has forgiven me. However, because she refuses to reconcile the relationship after much pleading on my part, I do not believe she has really forgiven me. Please tell me what steps I can take next to ensure that she has forgiven me and will reconcile our relationship.

T hank you for taking the time to share so many details of your heartbreaking story. Starting with the truth is the best place to solve situations. We were very sad as we read what you had to say because it is real, and happens more often than we care to admit. Our short response is that there is nothing we can tell you to help you reconcile with your girlfriend in the short run. Based on what you said, we believe your former girlfriend has forgiven you. Forgiving you and getting back together with you are two different issues. We suggest that you accept the fact your former girlfriend doesn't want to be your girlfriend anymore and move on. If you lied to your girlfriend before marriage, you will probably lie to your wife after you are married.

When it comes to relationships, rebuilding trust is among the most difficult realities to achieve. One of the legacies of our sinful natures is to remember the hurts of the past. As children, we learn not to put our hands on a hot stove because the consequences are cruel. So naturally, for the remainder of our lives, we will avoid touching hot stoves with our hands to keep from getting burned and feeling the pain that goes along with that experience. We believe because you are not married, your ex-girlfriend has chosen to move on and cut her losses rather than take a chance on someone who has already proven himself dishonest. Life is filled with choices and consequences. Once we make certain choices we cannot take them back. You seem to be reaping, in this instance, the fruit of your labor.

Please be assured that God forgives and has forgiven you if you have asked Him sincerely and determined in your mind to turn away from lying. You can also trust God to give you strength to follow through on that commitment so that your future relationships will reap the benefit of your newfound determination. Unless you take the time to ask God now to remove the sin of lying from your soul, you will continue to lie as a matter of habit, even into old age.

We hope you will choose the ways of God, and never forget that "righteous lips are the delight of kings; and they love him who speaks what is right" (Proverbs 16:13). You are in our prayers as you make this commitment every day for the remainder of your life.

A Strange Workout

A few weeks ago I woke up early in the morning and could not find my husband anywhere in the house. It was the day he doesn't work out, so I found it strange. Something told me to go out to the park, not far from our house, where he usually works out. When I got close to the park, I saw that my husband was working out with another woman. By the time I got to the park, the woman was in her car ready to take off. I ran up to the car and introduced myself to the woman as my husband's wife. She looked surprised and said my husband told her he was divorced. When I confronted him, he said he was sorry he had lied about our relationship, had just met the woman at work the day before, and nothing had happened between them. What advice do you have for me?

We are so sorry you had this experience. Despite the pain and shock this must have caused you, make no hasty decisions before having a calm and frank conversation with your husband. This is going to be very difficult. However, you both need to take stock of your relationship and identify, as best you can, what is happening in your marriage to cause your husband to behave in such a way. You should also engage the services of a professional counselor you both trust. If you don't know of any counselors, your pastor could be a good person to make a referral.

Infidelity, in any form, breaks the trust needed to sustain a marriage. While your husband may think he didn't cross that line, he has. Infidelity is a violation of the boundaries of an intimate relationship, betraying the core values upon which the integrity of the relationship is based. It describes an act of unfaithfulness to one's spouse or another person you are in a committed relationship with, whether sexual or nonsexual in nature.

We'll be quick to point out that you may have had nothing to do with the actions of your husband. While many suggest things don't happen in a vacuum, and that is true, you may not have caused the emptiness in your husband that led him to lie to a stranger about being married to you. Obviously, your husband has emotional wounds that led him to behave in a way that is harmful to your marriage.

Dr. Mark Laaser, a leading Christian psychologist, says in *The Seven Desires of Every Heart,* which he wrote with his wife, Debra: "If you did not have the desires met in your childhood, you may find unhealthy ways to get them met as an adult." It is important to note, since we are all humans with human parents or guardians who raised us and made mistakes, we are all wounded. While these wounds have left us with emotional gaps that may lead us to try to fill the void in our souls with something harmful to our families and ourselves, we must be mindful that only God can truly fulfill the desires of our hearts.

Psalm 37:4 states, "Delight yourself also in the LORD, and He shall give you the desires of your heart." This happiness that only Jesus can give, however, may never be fulfilled until we have fully explored our hurts with a professional Christian counselor who can help us come to grips with the pain from our past. We hasten to add, counseling is a spiritual gift given by God (1 Corinthians 12) to help build the body of Christ.

When we accept the healing of Jesus by calling on His name and allowing His Spirit to fill us, He will give us power to overcome the shortcomings in our lives. When this becomes a reality, we will bear the fruit of the Spirit (Galatians 5:22, 23).

We hope you will entrust your marriage to God and, together with your husband, experience the unity and joy that come only when you are willing to deal with your woundedness and emptiness. This takes place only when you allow the spiritual gifts God has given to transform your lives and give you the power to live honestly and victoriously in your marriage. We are praying for you.

Beyond Repair

I just found out that my husband has been unfaithful and has been having an affair for approximately six months. I am devastated and don't know what to do. I tried speaking to my husband about this issue, but he continues to ignore me. I told him we should see a counselor and try to fix things between us. I am willing to forgive him and put this behind us. However, he has moved out. We have been married for many years and have three children. Please help me.

Most married couples do not realize there is an unspoken agreement when they get married to fulfill each other's needs. While dating, men go all out to demonstrate their interest in, and love for, the woman they are pursuing. Frequent, and often long, telephone conversations (even after spending just several hours together) will occur. Romantic dinners and other outings are enjoyed on a regular basis. He might even bring her gifts to demonstrate his affection and concern for her happiness and well-being. The woman, invariably, reciprocates by falling deeply in love with this wonderful gentleman who is absolutely unbelievable, and accepts his offer of marriage with the assumption these incredible symbols of affection will continue for the remainder of their lives.

Unfortunately, most men, once married, get on with the pace of life, which is often too busy to include all the niceties of the past. Assumptions are made that the woman who is now married to him will understand these things are no longer important as they both take on greater responsibilities with marriage.

The truth is, successful marriages are based on reciprocity and a deep commitment to the well-being of the other. With every act of kindness and concern, each spouse makes deposits in the emotional bank account of the other. When this pattern of behavior ends, and there is no longer an intentional desire to make the other person happy, the lack of daily affirmation and attention becomes a withdrawal from the emotional bank account. When there are more emotional withdrawals than deposits made in these respective accounts, the relationship becomes overdrawn and soon becomes bankrupt.

When these realities take place in a marriage, regrettably, while emotional withdrawals are being registered by and from their respective spouses, emotional deposits are, customarily, being made to the spouse's account by someone outside of the marriage. Should these behaviors continue unchecked, eventually the emotional deposits made by the person outside of the marriage seem to pay off as an illicit relationship takes off. Although there is no biblical excuse for this type of behavior, the erring spouse often begins to believe he or she has the right to accept the affirmation and attention being provided by the outsider. After all, their husband or wife has not met their needs nor seems interested in doing so. Sad to say, because of these misunderstandings in marriage, research suggests 50 percent of Christian men are unfaithful to their wives.

At this point all you can do is appeal to your husband's Christian responsibility to you, his wife, and to the well-being of his children. Since you cannot force him to do anything, should he decide to continue his relationship with the other woman, you will need to accept his decision and move on.

We encourage you to find a highly recommended and qualified Christian counselor who can help you walk through this trauma and come to grips with what has taken place. This will help you to be in a position to offer emotional stability to your children and continue to live a productive and healthy life. Please know we are praying for you.

Truth and Consequences

Not long ago I had an affair. When my wife confronted me about the situation, I lied. She finally confronted the other woman and got the truth. We have two small children and a third on the way. My wife is angry, in pain, and says she feels betrayed. She often says she can never believe me again and wants a divorce. I am very sorry for what I did and wish this whole thing would just go away. I've told my wife several times that I am very sorry and that this will never happen again, but she doesn't believe me and keeps saying she feels betrayed. We went to a counselor, not a Christian, who told my wife divorce was an option if she could not trust me again. I don't want to lose my family. I love my wife and children and want us to stay together as a family. Please help me.

We are deeply sorry to hear about your situation, which is very delicate and difficult and will take quite a bit of work to repair. It is important for you to give your wife as much time as she needs. She feels betrayed, which is huge as far as the viability of your relationship is concerned. You need to allow her to calm down and keep reassuring her that you mean to keep your promises and tell the truth.

It is not wise for you to behave as if you are ready to leave what happened behind and get on with your lives. Your wife's perceptions of her marriage have been destroyed and will take some time for her to heal and believe in this marriage again. You are going to need to be genuinely sorry for what you did, and promise yourself and your wife that what you did will never happen again.

Your relationship will survive only if you give your wife reason to believe she can trust you again. What you did was like paying a million dollars for a piece of stale bread—too much for too little.

An affair is never worth the trouble it brings. It takes a man, however—a Christian man—to realize that marriage is serious business and takes commitment, maturity, and trust in God. The choices you make will bless or curse your family for generations to come. You must decide if you will pass on a legacy of faithfulness to your children or simply a model of how not to live one's life. While God forgives and brings peace, there are always consequences in sin.

Many believe—even Christians—that once an affair takes place in a marriage relationship there is no hope for that couple. We do not believe that. What we do believe is that marriage is sacred, and people who are married should purpose in their hearts, with God's help, never to break their marriage vows. However, if a spouse is unfaithful, while the Bible allows for divorce under those conditions, there is so much more at stake, especially in a family with children, that we would hope there could be genuine repentance, forgiveness, and reconciliation.

In Mark 10:2–9, the Bible says, "The Pharisees came and asked Him, 'Is it lawful for a man to divorce his wife?' testing Him. And He answered and said to them, 'What did Moses command you?' They said, 'Moses permitted a man to write a certificate of divorce, and to dismiss her.' And Jesus answered and said to them, 'Because of the hardness of your heart he wrote you this precept. But from the beginning of the creation, God "made them male and female." "For this reason a man shall leave his father and mother and be joined to his wife, and the two shall become one flesh"; so then they are no longer two, but one flesh. Therefore what God has joined together, let not man separate.' "

We suggest that you beg your wife—if you need to—for another opportunity to make it up to her and your children. Then find a good Christian counselor (go to www.adventistfamilyministries.com and click on Resources, then click on Directory of Counselors from the drop-down menu), and do what you must to save your marriage. You must promise yourself, and trust in the power of God, to keep you in the straight and narrow path of truth and faithfulness.

We hope you will recognize that only by staying close to Jesus and making up your mind to be faithful until death will you find what it takes to be true to your marriage and bring healing and peace to your family. We are praying for you.

Fixing a Busted Trust

What can a couple do to overcome infidelity, especially when the wife is having difficulty trusting?

Infidelity is one of the most devastating occurrences in any marriage. No doubt, God had a special reason for giving the seventh commandment— "you shall not commit adultery" (Exodus 20:14). God created marriage for our joy and blessing, and since God ordained marriage to be the closest and most intimate connection any human could have, He gave directives that would protect its sanctity and well-being.

Hebrews 13:4 states, "Marriage is honorable among all, and the bed undefiled; but fornicators and adulterers God will judge." This is God's way of reminding us that the marital vows are a holy commitment that should not be dishonored by anyone. We say all of this to establish that marriage is not only a cultural event we get involved with for our stability and to follow cultural norms, but also a holy institution that requires respect, responsibility, and commitment to our spouse and to God.

Invariably, affairs take place because there is emotional distance between marriage partners, and/or because one or both of them are not committed to being faithful to the marriage vows. Sometimes addictions are involved. However, in a large number of cases, inappropriate sexual involvement takes place because the necessary boundaries have not been put in place to avoid inappropriate relationships with other people.

To overcome infidelity, several things need to happen:

1. The person who has been unfaithful needs to recognize that what he or she has done is wrong and confess it to their partner. To do otherwise is to make matters more difficult since most times this kind of behavior will surface sooner than later and will further complicate the road to recovery.
2. The person who has been wronged needs to be given the time to fully explore the pain and concerns this inappropriate behavior has caused.
3. The offender needs to recognize how deeply his or her indiscretion has wounded the marriage and family, and ask for forgiveness.
4. The offended spouse has the choice to forgive or not forgive the offending spouse. If the slighted spouse does not allow himself or herself to forgive this offense, healing will not begin to take place, further complicating the process of overcoming infidelity.
5. If the offended partner agrees to forgive, the offender needs to show a determined commitment to not engage in this type of behavior in the future by pledging to develop appropriate boundaries with people he or she deals with.
6. The offended person needs to give herself or himself time to

heal. Despite forgiving your spouse of infidelity, the process of healing will take some time. The deeper the wound, given the circumstances of the infidelity, the more prominent the pain. Taking the time to see a well-recommended Christian counselor could be a good thing at this time.

7. The person who has been forgiven needs to give the offended party the necessary time to heal, sometimes even allowing that person to talk about the pain still being felt. It is the responsibility of the offender to behave in a way that will help rebuild the trust that was broken by their indiscretion.

Trust God to help you restore your marital relationship and use your pain as an opportunity for growth.

Remarriage and Social Security

My grandmother died last October. My grandfather is currently a deacon in his local church. He became close friends with a widow in his church he decided to marry. She will soon turn sixty and be eligible to receive Social Security benefits based on her former husband's benefits. She will not receive the Social Security if she remarries before the age of sixty. In order to not lose these benefits, my grandfather and his lady friend made vows before God and to each other privately, but have not been legally married. They are in the process of moving from their current church to another church where they are telling everyone they are married. They have also informed their current church they are married. Everyone assumes a judge performed a legal wedding, but my grandfather told me the true facts. This seems wrong to me, but I am not sure what should be done. Does the Bible accept this kind of marriage? If it doesn't, do I have a responsibility to do anything and inform anyone? Thank you for listening.

Your question is a very important one that keeps coming up quite often these days. We are pleased for your interest in doing the right thing and believe your conscience is alive and well by the concern you have shown about what is going on with your grandfather and his new "wife." However, we don't believe that it is up to you to do anything other than speak to your grandfather about your convictions concerning the situation he is in, and encourage him to do the right thing.

In Matthew 22:21, Mark 12:17, and Luke 20:25, Jesus says that we should give to Caesar what is Caesar's and to God what is God's. As Christians, it is our responsibility to be informed about the marriage laws of the state or country in which we live. In some countries, an ordained minister may perform the ceremony, as far as the civil authorities are concerned. However, the marriage contract has to be legally signed by the district registrar. In the United States, in so far as we know, in order to be legal, all marriages should be registered at the appropriate marriage bureau in the region (city, county, or state). And unless the request made by the state is against God's law, we should do what the law of the land says in order to live honest lives.

Your grandfather's wedding, as noble as it might be, fails the test of keeping the laws of the land, which Christians are called to do. When it comes to spiritual as well as legal issues, we cannot make up our own rules without bad consequences. We know that from a financial point of view, this is a very difficult issue for your grandfather and his new lady. However, you should remind your grandfather that this is an opportunity to put God to the test. If God has promised to "supply all your need" (Philippians 4:19), He surely can make up the difference for the lost Social Security income that your grandfather's new lady will experience.

Please know that we are praying for you, your grandfather, and his new lady, and hope you will allow the Spirit of God to lead you to use the right words to help your grandfather or anyone else do the right thing.

One Flesh

I am a Christian. For the last two months I have been in a relationship with a woman nine years my senior. She is a good Christian woman, with a missionary spirit that is inspiring. Together we make an awesome team in church. The problem is that when we are together outside of church we enter into sexual sin. Forgive me for being blunt about our situation. I just need you to understand what has happened to be able to help me with my question. While we haven't had intercourse with each other, we have engaged in very inappropriate conduct. Due to the unstable nature of our relationship, doubt, and sin, I have decided to end this relationship after receiving counsel from an elder of the church. He remarked, though, that if I had gone all the way with her then I would have to marry her. I do love her, and I would accept that responsibility wholeheartedly as a precept of God. Now, what I need you to clarify for me is, What do you have to do for God to consider you one with a woman? Does He consider us married already? Or is intercourse the only act that can obligate a union for life between two people?

Thank you for your question and especially for your honesty and what seems to be your sincere desire to do the right thing.

First, God considers two people one when they choose to be one through the commitment of marriage. The oneness referenced in Genesis 2:24, 25, is much more than mere physical oneness. Although having intercourse does appear to speak to the "one flesh" experience, the oneness here refers to the fact that Adam and Eve became complementary to each other, like two pieces in a puzzle, when they came together in marriage.

Second, forty-eight miles west of Athens, Corinth was a Greek city filled with temple prostitutes—male and female—who were a prominent part of the religious landscape, given the fact that in Greek philosophy there was belief in a distinct separation between the body and the spirit. The body was believed to be evil, and the spirit was believed to be good.

In this arrangement, the Corinthians engaged in sexual promiscuity at the temple and were considered still in good standing with their gods. In 1 Corinthians 6:15–18, the apostle Paul challenges the first-century believers, who had been raised with this wrong spiritual understanding, and points out to them that their bodies—every inch of them—were attached to Christ. Because they were attached to Christ, Paul declares, they could not possibly think about practicing immorality without being affected by it and grieving Christ. When Paul refers to this situation as "becoming one flesh" it wasn't so much to suggest that the man and the prostitute were one, as happens in marriage, but to point out the gravity of the sin and how much a believer would be affected by such an illicit relationship. In fact, Paul counseled believers to run away from this type of temptation.

Third, having shared the above, our answer is that we do not believe there is any act that obligates a union for life between two people, except for the commitment of marriage. Therefore, if you want to pursue a healthy and holy relationship with the woman you referenced, we counsel you to do so for the right reasons, and in the way God ordains it, or happiness and peace of mind will avoid you every single time.

Of course, the bigger issue here is the obvious guilt that you are feeling because of the inappropriate relationship you are having. In Romans 7:15–25, the apostle Paul makes clear that your situation is the problem of the human condition. Many times, as Christians, we do the very opposite of what we would like to do, just like the situation you have described. The answer to this problem, of course, is Jesus.

We hope you will understand your need of Christ's grace and power to overcome, and trust Him every day to deliver you from the sin over which you have no control. Remember, you can do all things through Him who strengthens you (Philippians 4:13), but you are going to have to rely on God to give you the victory.

Different Sexual Needs

I have been married for five years now, and I am often frustrated by the lack of sexual compatibility with my wife. She seldom seems to be interested in having intercourse when I am in the mood and never initiates sex. I want to be faithful to my wife, but her attitude is tempting me to look elsewhere for satisfaction. What do you suggest?

Your situation is not at all unusual. Most marriages, even successful ones, experience what you described above. The attitude you take when faced with this reality, and your awareness of the differences between men and women, is of great importance if your relationship is going to survive this concern.

While it is true that many accepted differences between men and women are socially constructed (society has arbitrarily decided that men and women should behave in certain gender-specific ways), the biochemical evidence of difference is overwhelming.

The fact that women have a menstrual cycle every twenty-eight days is a significant fact that you should always remember. Although it is true that not all women are affected in the same way or to the same degree during this monthly occurrence, there is some discomfort and loss of energy in almost every woman.

Another difference between men and women is that their emotions work very dissimilarly. While men crave—by their very nature—physical closeness, women crave, by their very nature, emotional closeness.

Since you have been married for five years, as stated in your question, we are going to assume that you probably have one or two children by now. If you do have children, they are obviously still very young and need lots of attention.

Our experience of almost seventeen years of marriage and family ministry, as well as the contemporary marriage literature, tells us that even in marriages in which husbands are committed to being an equal partner in house chores, in most cases the woman is still much more involved in taking care of the house and the children.

This reality, to be sure, comes with a price. Women who have young children are often extremely tired at the end of the day, especially if they are also involved in working outside the home, which is the case in most two-parent families in America, even those with younger children.

After a long day at work husbands and wives often come home to completely different scenarios. Wives usually pick up the children from day care or from the babysitter and are engaged in preparing the evening meal. Some husbands invariably sit back on the couch to watch the evening news or to read through the newspaper they didn't finish that morning.

By the time women get to bed, after cleaning up the kitchen and giving baths to children, they are often exhausted, with thought for little else other than sleep.

Therefore we would like to suggest that your wife is probably more tired than anything else. And she will probably continue to be tired for several years until the children become more self-sufficient.

Of course, this doesn't solve your dilemma. It is difficult for men to understand the matter of being tired to the point of not being interested in sexual intercourse, because this is often not the case for men. Since men are visual, even a tired wife in an old T-shirt can turn them on. Women, on the other hand, need to feel emotionally and spiritually close to their mate to be truly ready for intercourse.

Here are a few suggestions you may try in order to improve your situation: (1) Be sure to contribute as much as you can to the care of the children and house chores. This will conserve some of your wife's energies for other pursuits. (2) Be kind and loving to your wife all day, and flirt with her when you speak on the phone in the middle of the day. (3) Be intentional about planning your evening together to include great conversation, soft music, or other rituals that will set the mood. (4) Be sensitive, instead of demanding, and share with your wife your need to be physically close and intimate with her. (5) Express your love and appreciation for her and pray together for the good of your relationship. (6) Find strength in the Word of God that reminds us that God has promised to supply all of our needs.

If the above suggestions don't yield positive results, we suggest that you seek the help of a Christian counselor. Remember, you promised to love and cherish in sickness and in health. If there is obvious illness in the relationship, seek to get well together. Trust God, and do not allow Satan's temptations to ruin your life and the lives of your wife and children.

Healing From Infidelity

My husband cheated on me with another woman. We are now separated. How can I begin to get over the hurt and pain I am feeling?

Discovering that your spouse has been unfaithful is indeed a very painful experience and is devastating to marital oneness and intimacy. Hurt and anger are normal and healthy emotions to have after learning that your spouse has been unfaithful. You must give yourself time and space to think and evaluate the circumstances of your situation. Talk it through with a trusted, godly friend or a counselor. Verbalizing your hurt and anger is a healthy way of processing anger and working through the pain. Take the time to feel; do not be in a hurry to find hasty remedies, but allow yourself to identify and process the feelings you are having. Spend much time in prayer. Tell God how you are feeling and how deeply you have been hurt. Although He already knows your pain, admit your need for help from Him, and allow His peace to comfort and ease your pain.

Most important, ask God to give you the strength and the desire to forgive your spouse. Forgiveness is essential to your healing process. It is not at all an easy task, especially for the person who has been wronged, and it is not going to happen overnight. Nevertheless, when you forgive, your hurt heals, and you are released from the feelings of hatred, resentment, and bitterness that come from having been wronged. Forgiving is as much for your own sake as it is for the other person. When we forgive, God forgives us (Matthew 6:14). Forgiving does not excuse or justify the wrong committed by your spouse. However, when you forgive, you are relinquishing your right to retaliate. You are leaving vengeance to God (Romans 12:19), and leaving your hurt and painful memories at the foot of the cross.

Your best option is to find a Christian professional counselor who can help you and your spouse think clearly about what steps you will need to take next. Keep in mind that many relationships have been restored even when a spouse has been unfaithful. With God's help, restoration is an achievable goal for any couple who is willing to save their marriage. If your spouse is not willing to go to counseling, you should begin the process alone; it will help you process your own thoughts and feelings and help you in finding constructive ways to guide you through this situation. Our prayer is that the "peace of God, which transcends all understanding," will guard your heart and your mind during this season of your life (Philippians 4:7, NIV).

Sleeping With a Married Person

If I am sleeping with someone I am not married to, should I just ask for God's forgiveness? What should I do?

I f you are having a sexual relationship with someone you are not married to, asking God for forgiveness is a good first step in acknowledging the fact that you are indulging in sinful behavior. First John 1:9 clearly states, "If we confess our sins, he is faithful and just and will forgive us our sins and purify us from all unrighteousness" (NIV). So there is no question that forgiveness is available.

In addition to confessing to God, however, there are several subsequent steps you may want to consider in order to put this matter completely behind you:

- Tell the person you are sleeping with that you have decided to discontinue the behavior.
- Apologize to the individual you are sleeping with for contributing to his or her alienation from God.
- Recognize the natural cause-and-effect consequences of engaging in a sexual relationship outside of marriage. To that effect, Proverbs 6:27, 28 states, "Can fire be carried in the bosom without burning one's clothes? Or can one walk on hot coals without scorching the feet?" (NRSV).
- Follow the counsel of 1 Corinthians 6:18: "Flee sexual immorality [the Greek word for sexual immorality in this verse is *porneia,* or fornication]" (NIV). "Every sin that a person commits is outside the body; but the fornicator sins against the body itself" (NRSV). To be sure, this verse suggests that you do exactly what Joseph did when seduced by Potiphar's wife: run in the opposite direction as quickly as you can (Genesis 39:1–12).
- Consciously recommit your life and habits to the Lord. In the words of Romans 6:12, 13: "Therefore do not let sin reign in your mortal body so that you obey its evil desires. Do not offer any part of yourself to sin as an instrument of wickedness, but rather offer yourselves to God as those who have been brought from death to life; and offer every part of yourself to him as an instrument of righteousness."

Domestic Violence

Dangerous Turf

My husband is a good man. We have been married for about fifteen years. When I don't do exactly as he says, he gets really upset and sometimes hits me. It's not like he beats me up, like other women I hear about, but he might slap me once or push me. It has never gotten too out of control, but I am afraid that one of these days that will happen. What is your advice for me? Should I try to be more aware of his needs?

M arriage was created for companionship and the joy and blessing of the human race. In Genesis 1:31, the Bible states that at the end of God's creative work, which included the creation of Adam and Eve, "then God saw everything who He had made, and indeed it was very good." The wisest man who ever lived, Solomon, declares in Proverbs 5:18: "Rejoice with the wife of your youth."

It is not difficult to observe that God meant marriage to be a wonderful relationship between a man and a woman. And to make things even clearer, 1 Peter 3:7 declares, "Husbands, likewise, dwell with them with understanding, giving honor to the wife, as to the weaker vessel, and as being heirs together of the grace of life, that your prayers may not be hindered."

While Peter took more time instructing wives than husbands, because of the new reality Christianity brought to women who were kept down in the Roman Empire, here he speaks to husbands about the fundamentals of marriage. Four areas of importance are highlighted in this text: the physical, intellectual, emotional, and spiritual. Your question deals specifically with the physical, and the message from God's Word is clear; husbands should relate to their wives with understanding, honor, and grace, so that they can be on good terms with God. The physical element of the text is in the words "dwell with them," which is much more than simply sharing the same address, but becoming one flesh (Ephesians 5:31) and having authority over each other's bodies (1 Corinthians 7:4) in the context of caring for each other.

Nowhere in Scripture are men given authority to behave other than respectfully and with love toward their wives. No matter how good a man your husband is, he has no right to beat or push you, even if he thinks you have not done exactly as he said. God is clear that if husbands do not treat their wives as the weaker vessel (we understand this is not always literally the case) their access to God will be hindered.

At a more basic level, nothing you do justifies the treatment you described above. You cannot change your husband's behavior. It is his responsibility to get professional help to ensure this does not happen again. Apologies and promises, apart from treatment, will not end the violence in your home. The present situation needs to stop immediately and be addressed, so that your home will be a place of safety for you and your children.

Trust God for strength and the willingness to deal with the difficult issues in your marriage, so that your family might be the kind of witness that will draw people to Jesus.

Domestic Violence

Every time I hear someone talk about domestic violence, especially in church, I feel that men are being bashed and made to feel guilty. I think that men are abused as much as women. What do you think?

We are pleased to hear that some of our churches are bringing attention to this social dilemma. Many people believe that communities of faith are exempt from this problem; unfortunately, they are not.

First, let's define domestic violence and abuse. It usually refers to a pattern of violent and coercive behavior exercised by one person over another in an intimate relationship (e.g., husband-wife, boyfriend-girlfriend, parent-child). It is not just marital conflict or a "lover's" quarrel. It may consist of repeated severe beatings or more subtle forms of abuse, including threats, intimidation, and psychological control.

In a direct answer to your question, yes, there are incidents of men being abused.

However, statistics reflect that 95 percent of domestic violence victims are women. Some critics say that is because women report more incidents of abuse than men do. No matter who is being victimized, domestic violence is a serious problem and must be addressed, especially by our church family.

There is no need for anyone to feel bashed or pity when the issue of abuse surfaces—unless, of course, the person is guilty. The goal here is healing for both the abused and the abuser. Skip the feelings of guilt and become an advocate for peace and healing in your local church. Encourage your pastor to speak out more against violence and abuse. Support and/or participate in awareness programs about the topic; designate a day or month for educating and activating the congregation.

If someone you know tells you they are being abused, listen to them and believe them. Rarely is such abuse contrived. Let them know that abuse is not God's will for them, and assure them that you are willing to help them seek shelter or intervention.

If you believe that you are a victim of domestic violence and abuse, you must immediately seek help, safety, or shelter. Talk with someone you trust or call the National Domestic Violence Hotline (800-799-SAFE or 7233) for help from a local domestic violence program. Trust your instincts and recognize that abuse is not your fault. If you choose to remain in the situation for now, set up a safety plan of action (e.g., set aside some money and maybe a car key in a safe place and find somewhere to go in case of an emergency).

If you believe yourself to be a potential batterer—you are extremely jealous, you try to control your spouse's or girlfriend's activities, you believe that as head of the household you should not be challenged, or you use physical force to solve problems—then you are probably hurting the people you love. You should get help right away from someone who will hold you accountable. It takes much courage, but you are not alone. As Christians, we have a moral obligation to be conduits of God's love, peace, and healing. "Let us therefore make every effort to do what leads to peace and to mutual edification" (Romans 14:19, NIV).

Emotional Abuse

I often hear people speak about emotional or psychological abuse. While I believe that physical violence is easy to define, it seems that emotional abuse is much more subjective, and could be used to describe or manipulate almost any situation. Are there really any objective indicators of emotional abuse?

Abuse is any behavior that is designed to control and subjugate another human being through the use of fear, humiliation, intimidation, guilt, coercion, manipulation, and so on. Emotional abuse is any kind of abuse that is emotional rather than physical in nature. It can include anything from verbal abuse and constant criticism to more subtle tactics such as repeated disapproval, or even the refusal to ever be pleased.

Emotional abuse is like brainwashing in that little by little it wears away at the victim's self-confidence, sense of self-worth, trust in his or her own perceptions, and self-concept. Whether it is done by constant belittling, by intimidation, or under the guise of "guidance," "teaching," or "advice," the results are similar. Eventually, the recipient of the abuse loses all sense of self and remnants of personal value.

Emotional abuse cuts to the very core of a person. This kind of abuse leaves scars that may be far deeper and more lasting than physical ones. With emotional abuse, the insults, insinuations, criticism, and accusations slowly eat away at the victim's self-esteem until he or she is incapable of judging the situation realistically. The person who has been emotionally abused is so emotionally beaten down that he or she will blame himself or herself for the abuse.

Victims of emotional abuse find that it is difficult to name or even talk about. They often wonder if it is serious because you cannot see it, like the bruises, black eyes, or broken bones of physical abuse. One of the biggest problems emotionally abused people face is that others seldom take it seriously. While emotional abuse might be difficult to pinpoint, there are definitely some objective indicators one can look for. The following questions will help you identify some of the signs of emotional abuse:

- What is your relationship like? Do you feel that something is wrong with your relationship but you don't know how to describe it?

- Do you feel that the person controls your life?
- Do you feel that the person does not value your thoughts or feelings?
- Will the person do anything to win an argument, such as put you down, threaten you, or intimidate you?
- Will the person get angry and jealous if you talk to someone else? Are you often accused of having affairs?
- Do you feel that you cannot do anything right in the person's eyes?
- Do you have to account for every moment of your time?
- Does the person blame you for everything that goes wrong?
- Are you unable or afraid to make decisions for yourself?
- Do you do anything you can out of fear to please the person or to not upset him or her?
- Do you make excuses for the person's behavior?
- Are you forgetful, confused, or unable to concentrate?
- Have you lost interest or lack energy to do the things you used to do?
- Do you feel sick, anxious, tired, or depressed a lot of the time?
- Have you lost contact with your friends, family, or neighbors?
- Have you lost self-confidence and feel afraid that you could not make it alone?

If the answer is yes to many of the questions above, then emotional abuse might be present in your relationship. It's important for you to realize that emotional abuse is a serious problem, and anyone in this situation (abuser or abused) should seek help from a trained mental-health professional. Don't give up if your first attempt at getting help is not taken seriously. Continue to look for someone who knows how to recognize the signs of emotional abuse and will take this form of abuse seriously. Emotional abuse is as bad as, or worse, than physical abuse, and in many cases emotional abuse can lead to physical abuse.

We hope that now you will be better able to identify the presence of emotional abuse and that God will empower you to be an advocate for those who find themselves in this situation.

Living in an Abusive Relationship

I have been in an abusive relationship with a well-respected professional and church member. I have a two-year-old son who has seen his father abuse me at least three times. I have suffered from beatings, chokings, humiliation, bruises, and more. I left this time even though things were going great for the past four months. Now I am feeling as if I made a big mistake. I told him that he would have to go to marriage counseling or we would get a divorce. He kept giving me the runaround, so the next day I packed up all that I could and left. Please, I need help. I am twenty six years old, and I have nothing. He has the house, cars, a good job, and so on. In our first year together I was arrested for attempted aggravated assault with a deadly weapon despite the fact that I had bruises and he had none. He had filed a false report on me before, but a female detective saw right through him. Anyway, I didn't fight it and served probation. I cannot find a decent job now. Am I wrong? Should I have stayed and prayed? I felt as though I was dying there. I no longer want to be with anyone who has done these things to me, even if he's changed and become the sweetest man in the world. Please help. I need answers quickly. Thank you.

We feel pained for what you have been going through and hope that soon you may get the help that you so desperately need and are asking for. People in your situation often choose to suffer in silence rather than reaching out for help.

Unfortunately, the abuse of women and also men, takes place with regularity around the world. There is no specific profile of an abuser. They come in every age, size, race, ethnicity, class, occupation, and religion. The fact that a man is a church member, professional (or not professional), and to all appearances a nice man, does not mean he is not abusing the woman or women (daughters, granddaughters, nieces, sisters, mother, and so on) in his life.

Abusive behavior is a disease that often afflicts men (and also women) who themselves have suffered some type of abuse during the early part of their lives. There is no good excuse or explanation, however, for why a person abuses others, although abusers are quick to give what they believe are good reasons why they abuse loved ones. We want to be quick to say here that no one deserves to be abused no matter what they have or have not done. And, by the way, abuse occurs in cycles, usually caused by an incident (almost anything) that triggers the abusive behavior, immediately followed by apologies or gifts (chocolate, flowers, and so on), and promises that it will never happen again. And sometimes it feels that the promise made by the abuser has been kept—sometimes for several months (possibly for even more than four months)—until another incident occurs that triggers the abusive behavior all over again. And the cycle goes on and on.

You described the classic symptoms of someone experiencing abuse. Your situation, nevertheless, won't get better until your husband can admit his problem and get professional help. Your first order of business is to be in a safe place for yourself and your child. We are especially concerned about your young son who has experienced your abuse, and by so doing has also been abused himself. We would encourage you to call the National Domestic Violence Hotline immediately at 800-799-7233 (open seven days a week, twenty-four hours a day). The hotline will connect you with people in your area who can be of assistance to you and help you navigate the difficult situation you find yourself in, including legal help if you have that need.

One of the biggest mistakes made by people, especially church people, is to be in denial about what happened or is happening to them. They are often embarrassed, don't want anyone else to know about the abuse, and are often protective of their abuser's reputation if that person is an important person in the church (pastor, elder, deacon, and so on), in the business world, or in some other type of public work. Silence, however, is not the appropriate response in these types of situations. The quicker this matter comes to light, the easier it is for the malady to be dealt with and for the wrong to be made right.

Trust God to lead you and to help put your family back together. Prayer alone, however, won't do it. People who are doing wrong must admit their wrong, repent, get professional help, and be safe in order for their spouse and children to live without fear.

Parenting

The New Conversation About Race

My husband and I are concerned about how to approach the topic of race and racism with our children. As African-American Christian parents of boys who are eight and ten years of age, my husband and I want to be sure they understand clearly our need to love everyone. At the same time, our country has had a violent history of racism that has not altogether disappeared despite the election of an African American as president of the United States. We want to be sure our boys have a strong self-esteem and identity without hating anyone because of their ethnicity or national origin. Do you have any counsel for us?

One of the most challenging jobs any human being will have to do is that of parenting children to be positive and productive members in the family, society, and the church. Parents are the key to whether the next generation will contribute positively to the public discourse and behavior in civil society.

The issues of race and racism are among the most difficult to communicate with our children about because these are issues filled with pain, and even feelings of hatred, for many of us as people of color. The truth is that unless we have come to grips with the issues of race and racism for ourselves, we will not be able to pass on a healthy perspective to our children.

Racism, according to Dictionary.com, is "a belief or doctrine that inherent differences among the various human racial groups determine cultural or individual achievement, usually involving the idea that one's own race is superior and has the right to dominate others."

When we looked for the definition of *race* in Dictionary.com, other than referring to the concept of "a contest of speed, as in running, riding, driving, or sailing," there was no other notion that denotes the issue we are dealing with. In Wikipanion, however, we found the following definition: "Race and ethnicity in the United States Census as defined by the Federal Office of Management and Budget (OMB) and the United

States Census Bureau are self-identification data items in which residents choose the race or races with which they most closely identify, and indicate whether or not they are of Hispanic or Latino origin (ethnicity)."

Social science usually defines race as "socially constructed." In other words, it is a concept made up by human beings to classify and determine differences between peoples. After all, it is very difficult today to find someone in American society who is 100 percent of any racial group.

The Bible text that seems most applicable in this context is Matthew 10:16, which states, "Behold, I send you out as sheep in the midst of wolves. Therefore *be wise as serpents and harmless as doves*" (emphasis added).

The truth is, as people of God, our behavior and the way we raise our children need to be compatible with the biblical ethic of loving our neighbors as we love ourselves. The way we talk about others in the privacy of our homes will be manifested in public by the way our children behave—when we least expect it.

Trust God to help you live right no matter the response of others. You and your family will continue in our prayers.

Prayers for Kids That Get Answered

Last year my son was arrested; my daughter is disrespectful to her dad and me and doesn't seem to be interested in church or God. I pray constantly for my kids, and yet sometimes I wonder if God hears my prayers. I feel so hurt and hopeless as I see my kids drifting away from the ways we taught them, and from God. Does God really hear and answer prayers?

As parents ourselves, we are touched personally by your question. Each day we pray, pleading on behalf of our children for God to protect them and save them in His kingdom. We want to assure you that God hears and answers prayers (Matthew 7:7).

There are many reasons people, especially parents, question the effectiveness of their prayers. These reasons may include guilt, fear, helplessness, and hopelessness. We might admit that when our kids don't turn out the way we raised them, we somehow feel that perhaps God is punishing us for something we did, or something we didn't do right with them. That guilt leads to worshiping God out of fear instead of a true and honest relationship with our heavenly Father.

The wonderful thing about God is that He is love! He loves us "with an everlasting love" (Jeremiah 31:3). We are also reminded in 1 John 4:18: "There is no fear in love; but perfect love casts out fear, because fear involves torment. But he who fears has not been made perfect in love." Don't allow guilt, fear, and anxiety about punishment to cripple you as a parent.

God is a loving parent who longs for us to enter into a deep and real relationship with Him. He wants us to understand who He is as a parent, so we can then know how to parent our children. He definitely knows firsthand what it is like to see a child in anguish and pain. He sent His own Son to earth as a human being to experience pain and suffering on our behalf (John 3:16). Jesus reacted much the same as we do when He asked three times if there was another way. He also displayed a sense of human abandonment when He exclaimed: "My God, My God, why have You forsaken Me?" (Mark 15:34).

Perhaps our difficulty with praying is that we can accept God's "Yes," but we have difficulty with His "No" or His "Wait." One way to learn how to accept the negative or wait answers is to keep record of all the positive answers we've received. Has God been good to you? Has He answered any of your prayers? Can you think of any blessings you have received from Him? Do you have anything to be thankful for?

God's promises are true! He is faithful! Memorize His promises, such as Philippians 4:6, 7: "Be anxious for nothing, but in everything by prayer and supplication, with thanksgiving, let your requests be made known to God; and the peace of God, which surpasses all understanding, will guard your hearts and minds through Christ Jesus."

God wants us to cry out to Him daily. When we pray, our prayers should not be filled only with demands but with praise and thanksgiving. The more we praise, the more we are reminded of God's love, grace, and mercy. Our prayers do make a difference; praying changes not only our circumstances, but most important, praying changes us. Prayer draws us closer to God, so "pray without ceasing" (1 Thessalonians 5:17). The closer we draw to God, the more we are convicted that He indeed hears and answers our prayers every day and always.

Ultimately, your children will have to choose for themselves to live by the values you taught them. Keep praying for them, trusting God to reveal Himself to them. Hopefully they will choose to follow God, but no matter what they choose, continue to love your children unconditionally, just as God loves you.

Dating Too Soon

Our children are encouraged by the public school system to begin dating at a very early age. The dances and other activities that are organized to get the students paired off with someone of the opposite sex seem to push them into intimate relationships before they are ready for them. What counsel do you have for parents who are concerned about the potential problems these organized activities may cause our children?

Ours is an overstimulated culture that pushes children to explore the transitions to adolescence in ways that are often less than adequate for their present and future well-being. In their attempt to help preteens and teens explore the early stirrings of sexual attraction, school systems integrate certain activities to create an outlet for the exploration of these attractions.

We would like to make two points on this issue for your consideration and that of our other readers: (1) Parents have the option to choose where to send their children to school. (2) Parents can determine what activities their children may or may not participate in.

On the first issue we believe that children are a gift from God. The Bible states, "Lo, children are an heritage of the LORD: and the fruit of the womb is his reward" (Psalm 127:3, KJV). Because this is so, parents should do all they can to give their children the best opportunities possible. This may include sending their children to church school where the values that are taught are values that parents believe in. This kind of environment makes it easier to allow children to participate in the social activities.

We would be the first to agree that it is rather expensive to send children to church school. However, we challenge you to put God to the test, since He has promised to supply all of your needs (Philippians 4:19). Allow God to work miracles for you and your children and in the process exercise your muscle of faith.

On the second issue we believe that it is the privilege of parents to decide what activities their children will participate in. Just because the school system is involved in organizing social activities for the students does not mean that parents should allow their children to participate. If the activity organized at the school is not compatible with the parents' values, it would be irresponsible for them to allow their children to participate.

We believe that one of the best things parents can do to foster a healthy social life for their preteens and teens is to organize activities in their homes where friends can be invited to have a good time under the supervision of the parents. Of course, the older the teen becomes, which also means there is greater maturity and responsibility, the more privileges that young person may have. However, fostering an environment where there is serious dating going on between preteens and teens still in high school is simply premature and setting up young people to "practice divorcing" and getting their feelings hurt unnecessarily. At this age most young people are not emotionally mature enough to sustain long-lasting dating relationships, and invariably break up and go on to another boyfriend or girlfriend.

Trust God to help you guide your children for present and future success, especially in their intimate relationships.

Don't Give Up

We are truly concerned about the behavior of our children these days. We have two children: a girl, age sixteen, and a boy, age fourteen. We know the teen years are usually more challenging than the earlier years. However, it appears that teenagers are becoming much more difficult than they have ever been. Is it something we are doing wrong? Please help us to understand what is going on. We really love our children, but their recent bad behavior is much more than we signed on for.

Parenting is one of the most challenging, satisfying, and important jobs on earth. At best, children are a work in progress, filling us with pride as they develop each day in front of our eyes. At worst, children can be the most mentally challenging reality of our existence.

The ideal is to raise children to be independent enough to eventually take care of themselves, while connected enough to look to their respective families for guidance and support. The best-case scenario is for children to have a balance—neither complete independence, nor complete dependence, but an ideal reality called interdependence.

Most people who become parents are not really prepared for the shock their lives will experience with this new situation. No one should have to go through this life-altering experience without being in a committed marriage partnership. Once you have children, it affects every aspect of your life—your time, activities, priorities, hobbies, career, education, and friends. All take a back seat to the new life you are now responsible for.

Without knowing it, we often take shortcuts in the process of raising our children because we don't realize that it is going to be so demanding. We spend less time with them than they need. We convince ourselves we love all of our children the same—after all, we give them all the same things—while they are different individuals with different needs, who will respond differently to the same treatment.

More often than not, most parents don't get training to be excellent parents; rather, they default to the way they were parented, without realizing what worked for them is not working for their child, who may have a completely different personality and temperament than they.

The more training in good parenting we have, the more aware we will be of what our individual children need, and this will give us an opportunity to give the effort of parenting the best attention, and probably get the best results.

There is at least one other thing parents of difficult children can do to advantage themselves; choose a positive attitude in dealing with them. The Word of God states in Proverbs 15:13: "A merry heart makes a cheerful countenance, but by sorrow of the heart the spirit is broken."

Trust God to save your family, and by so doing, feel healthier, happier, and at peace with God's promise to supply whatever you need (Philippians 4:19).

Shaky Ground

I suspect my nineteen-year-old daughter is drinking alcohol. When I confronted her about it, she became very angry and denied it. How do I deal with this issue to be of greatest help to her?

One of the most difficult issues parents have to deal with is seeing their children experimenting with risky behaviors. To be sure, one of the trademarks of today's teenagers is their sense of adventurism, which will most certainly backfire if it is left unchecked.

When it comes to alcohol, teens are particularly vulnerable to its use. The developmental changes they are going through often make them feel self-conscious and more likely to take risks, such as experimenting with alcohol and other drugs. They may do so to please others or to fit in, or just because they are curious and want to try something new.

As teens get older and are of college age, there is even greater peer pressure to use alcohol as a form of celebration, or to create excitement and an illusion of having fun. They are greatly influenced by societal messages or media images of people drinking alcohol as a form of socializing. Many people will say alcohol is simply a "social" beverage. However, in actuality, alcohol is a psychoactive drug (meaning it alters our feelings, our thoughts, our perceptions of the world, and our behavior).

Teens may also experiment with alcohol because they feel rejected by their parents or other family members, or from lack of parental guidance. Researchers have found the most consistent nondrinkers have sound relationships with their parents, have good parental monitoring, and have more fear of disappointing their parents than they do of their discipline.

To increase your success in having a meaningful conversation with your daughter, choose a time you are both relaxed and calm. Don't use that as an excuse to delay the conversation for too long or to not have the discussion. Even if she denies using alcohol, by broaching the topic you will help give her the guidance and support necessary to make good choices.

When you begin, try not to lecture her (this is extremely hard for parents), and try not to appear judgmental. You might begin by asking about her views on drinking—find out what she knows and thinks about alcohol. Then you can share some facts with her, such as the fact that alcohol is a drug and is a depressant, not a stimulant. It gives the appearance of making one happy or popular, but in reality can cause sadness and anger. Alcohol slows the mind and the body, and anyone can develop an alcohol problem—even a teen without risk factors for alcohol abuse. Discuss reasons not to drink, and help her plan ways to handle peer pressure. Also remind her of, or establish house rules and consequences about, alcohol and drug use and enforce them consistently.

Most important, however, is to strengthen your relationship with your daughter and to help her strengthen her relationship with Jesus Christ. Help her understand that no matter what she is going through, real power and strength will come from having a personal relationship with Christ and not from alcohol and other drugs. Talk to her often so you can continue to pass on your values to her.

It is our prayer that from this day forward you will put your daughter in God's hands daily and allow Him to lead you both to a stronger and healthier relationship in Him and with each other.

Note: If you notice significant mood changes or behavior problems in your teen, contact your teen's doctor or a counselor who specializes in alcohol problems.

Grieved and Resentful

I am grieved to no end at the behavior of my young adult son who has been home during the summer vacation after his first year in college. He goes and comes as he pleases in the car my husband and I have given him, and he thinks he doesn't have to tell us anything about his whereabouts. He comes in at all hours of the night and early morning without telling us where he is going, with whom, or what time he will be home. I often stay up very late worrying about his safety. Should I accept this behavior as a fact of his age, or should I share my feelings and concerns with him? I am resentful and feel like I am losing my mind.

There is no doubt in our minds that after marriage, parenting is probably one of the most challenging relationships to manage in life. The difference with parenting is that we cannot easily pass the buck and say that we had nothing to do with the way a particular person was raised. Our children, to a great extent, are who we nurture them to be. However, because there are no perfect parents, neither are there perfect children, teens, or young adults. In addition, the training we give our children is often not visible in their behavior until their midtwenties or even later.

Being aware of the developmental stages every relatively normal child is likely to go through can make things easier in the relationship between us and our growing and maturing children.

One of the most difficult, and at once most challenging, times in life is when parents are in middle age and children are teenagers. In midlife we often experience rapid, but not necessarily welcome, change. On top of all this, we are feeding, clothing, housing, and educating children who are in their mid to late teens who feel grown, want to be left alone to do their own thing, and sometimes behave like ingrates.

Based on biblical principles and sheer common sense, we believe that every privilege comes with responsibility. Our children, including our college-age teenagers and young adults who still live in our homes, enjoy many privileges we provide for them every day. Their corresponding responsibility is to live by the house rules we have set, which need to be reasonable, age-appropriate, and Christian.

We love and respect our children, and we expect love and respect in return. We inform each other where we will be and when we plan to return home. While we no longer have a curfew in our home, we have a house rule that makes it clear what the latest time is that any member of our family will arrive at home each evening (or host guests at home). If an hour before the deadline or anytime thereafter it appears that we will not be home at the appointed time, we call, get in touch, explain our situation, and have an agreement on how to proceed.

While our daughter and son are not always ecstatic about this reality, they know the day will come when they will pay their own way and go and come as they please. At that time, they will be happy to be accountable to their respective spouses or to a good friend. Young people who do not learn to be accountable to their parents will not do so well being accountable to their spouses, and life will be an uphill climb every step of the way.

The Bible states in Ephesians 6:1: "Children, obey your parents in the Lord, for this is right."

We hope you will agree to sensible boundaries in your family that will help you keep your sanity and prepare your children for a life of accountability and success as responsible adults.

Having the Talk!

Can you give me some suggestions on how to begin talking with my eight- and ten-year-old about sex?

We applaud you for wanting to be intentional about speaking to your children about healthy sexuality. For many parents this is a frightening task; for obvious reasons speaking intimately about sexuality makes people embarrassed and uncomfortable. When Adam and Eve committed the first sin, they immediately felt naked and ashamed (Genesis 3:6, 7); one consequence of their sin was sexual shame. So accept discomfort as a natural part of the process.

Sexuality education is a part of character and moral education; not only do you want to teach your children about "where babies come from," but you want them to develop healthy, biblical values about sex, love, and marriage. First, you (and your spouse) must explore your own attitudes toward sex. Modeling healthy male-female relationships is equally as important as what you actually say to your children. Perhaps you have not had "the conversation" yet, but you have already communicated messages to them about sexuality by your own response to sexuality. You will be much better prepared to speak to your children about this topic if you are willing to examine your beliefs and feelings about sex. Naturally, once you begin examining your attitudes, certain voices from your past may try to convince you that you are not qualified to teach anyone about healthy sexuality.

If this happens, ignore these voices and look to God, who has promised you strength, power, forgiveness, and healing from whatever challenges may arise. If it seems that it is more than you can handle on your own, seek out the assistance of a qualified pastor or Christian counselor. Please keep in mind that you do not have to be perfectly whole to speak to your children about sex. But the more comfortable you are with your own sexuality, the more comfortable you will be talking to your children about it.

One of the least threatening ways to start talking to children about sexuality is by using a "facts of life" book; this provides a comfortable door-opener for conversation. When your children ask you questions about sex, do not be afraid to answer truthfully; just remember to be age-appropriate. Don't give more information than your children can process at their age. Use teachable moments, such as seeing a pregnant woman, a couple getting married, a television program that shows certain attitudes or values about sex (even if you do not watch it), anything that can initiate a discussion. These discussions do not have to wait until you are privately sequestered somewhere, but can happen right at the dinner table or during family worship. We pray that you will be empowered and encouraged as you prepare yourself to educate your children about what God has ordained for human beings to cherish and enjoy.

Communicating With Teenagers

My husband and I recently attended one of your workshops and learned a lot about how to communicate effectively with each other. We are making progress in our relationship, but our teenagers really have a problem communicating properly with us and with each other. Should our children attend a workshop to learn how to communicate with us?

We are pleased to know that you went to one of our workshops and found our segment on communicating effectively to be helpful. We have discovered for ourselves that inviting God to be in charge of our marriage each day is extremely beneficial. The other piece of the equation, however, is learning to do what God says. The Bible is clear that everyone should "be swift to hear, slow to speak, slow to wrath" (James 1:19). The communication skills we teach are based on the principles of this Bible text.

People at every stage of life can benefit from learning to communicate well. Even children and teenagers can learn much about communicating effectively. Sending some teens to a workshop to learn to communicate, though, is like telling them to eat their vegetables so that their minds and bodies will be strong and healthy. Chances are they will not easily do so because we say so, unless it has been a part of their daily routine while growing up. They may perceive our sending them to participate in this kind of event as a criticism of them, and completely ignore the training out of rebellion.

On the other hand, the Bible does say: "Train up a child in the way he should go" (Proverbs 22:6). The Hebrew word for "train" is "dedicate."

However, only in this text is the verb translated "train." The Hebrew word seems to incorporate the idea of setting aside, tightening, or putting a hedge around something. The word is occasionally used to imply the beginning of something. The training of children involves showing them godly behavior that moves them away from evil as a habit in their lives. This is the work of parents, more so than the job of teachers or other instructors. To get our children to learn how to communicate in a healthy manner, we need to model healthy communication by the way we speak to each other and by the way we speak to them.

Home should be a holy place in a child's life, a place where supreme love and acceptance are found between parents and with the children. The real assessment of a parent's spirituality is his home life—whether or not he shows a character like Christ's. Our responsibility goes beyond feeding, clothing, and putting a roof over our children's heads to nurturing their minds, their spirits, and their values. By what we say to them as well as by our personal example, we have to carefully guide our children and earnestly make an effort to show them what it means to be like Jesus. Good parenting, then, also involves making sure there is healthy communication among all the members of the family. For this to happen, however, family members need to spend quality time talking to each other every day, playing together, having daily family worship, as well as making weekly church attendance a regular exercise the entire family engages in to acknowledge the God they believe in and serve.

We believe that your children, and children in general, will learn to communicate well and a lot easier when the significant adults in their lives communicate with patience, caring, and understanding. When we create an environment of love, forgiveness, and acceptance, it becomes the frame of reference our children have and more likely the way they will behave.

Determine to use every day the communication skills you learned at our workshop. This will fill your home with the sweet savor of the Spirit of God and help make it a little heaven on earth.

The Pleasures and Pain of Parenthood

I have three young children, and for the most part I am just tired and upset all the time. My oldest child is a son who is seven. I thought that by now he would be a bigger help with the other children so I can take care of the other kids. Instead he just makes me angry when he acts like he needs more help from me. I sometimes scream at him out of frustration so that he can get it, but things are not changing; in fact, they are going from bad to worse. What can I do to make things better?

Thank you for your honest question and for recognizing the possibility of a better way to reach your seven-year-old son. We believe you can help your son to improve at an age-appropriate pace, and at the same time help yourself to feel better about your circumstances.

Parenting is one of the great blessings in life, but at the same time it can be one of the most difficult burdens to bear if you do not have realistic expectations about the progress children should be making at a particular stage of their lives. The burden seems even heavier if there is no help from your spouse—if you have one—or from other relatives and friends to get the job done.

To improve your current circumstances and make things better, you need to first realize that one of the most important things you can do for your children is to help them develop a positive attitude about life. It is a lot easier for your children to have an upbeat mind-set when they have strong self-esteem. A positive self-esteem is necessary for children, and also for adults, to feel good about their circumstances, even if things are not perfect around them. Children and adults have a positive self-esteem when they feel loved, accepted, and capable.

At the age of seven, your oldest child is still very young and needs your help with many things, even though he is older than the other two children. He needs to feel loved, accepted, affirmed, and supported by you. The more you encourage and affirm your son about the small improvements he makes with things he does around the house, the more capable, loved, respected, valued, and sure of himself he will feel. The more you believe in your son, the more he will believe in himself.

One of the biggest challenges in families is to learn how to develop a positive atmosphere in the home among family members. The less we nag and the more we praise and affirm our children for their efforts, the brighter, happier, and more constructive our family environment will be. For this to happen, parents must be intentional about creating this kind of place for their families. Instead of paying attention only to the mistakes children make, parents need to be quick to point out the good things children accomplish in their everyday lives. The more you respect your son around the house by not yelling at him and putting him down, the more capable you will make him feel and the better you will feel about the way things are going around your house.

We hope you will remember God's promise to be with you always (Matthew 28:20) and to supply all of your needs (Philippians 4:19). Trust Him and claim these promises on behalf of yourself and your children, and you will enjoy a newfound positive spirit and environment in your home.

Parent and Teenager Challenges

My teenager is driving me crazy. She is rude, ungrateful, and always in a bad mood. I am a single parent trying to do my best to provide for my children by working two jobs. By now, I expected to be getting help from my sixteen-year-old, but she is even worse than her ten-year-old sister. What can I do to turn things around? Please help me.

As parents of teenagers, we empathize with your situation. If it makes any difference, please know that most parents of teenagers share your experience, although some have a slightly better time than others. The teen years are among the most difficult in the life of any person because it is a time when they are trying to find out who they are and are trying to establish independence from their parents.

Teens go out of their way to try to be different from their parents. Teens try to be different from their parents by the music they listen to, the language they speak (they use slang that is constantly changing and meant to be different than the language of adults), the fads they are caught up with, the clothes they wear, and the exclusive relationships they develop with people of the opposite sex, and sometimes with people of the same sex, that make them feel special.

One of the main reasons teenagers have conflict with their parents is that they go out of their way to be different from their parents. Teenagers want to be their own persons, and tend to identify with people their age—classmates, friends from their neighborhoods, rappers, other celebrities, and even friends from church—rather than with people who are sacrificing to put food on their tables, clothes on their backs, and a roof over their heads.

The language you used to describe your teenager is quite accurate. Since teenagers want to do exactly the opposite of what their parents expect them to do, they appear rude when they communicate their lack of interest in their parents' suggestions. They are likely to say, "You can go ahead and do it that way, but I am not interested." It is their way of trying to be independent and to be their own person. Because teenagers are in that stage of life where they lack maturity and good judgment, and are still in the process of becoming responsible human beings, they will often be in a bad mood when they are around their parents who are trying to get them to do something different than they want to do.

This means that teenagers who behave the way you described are behaving normally. If you can remember this when dealing with your teenager, it will be easier for you not to take her behavior too personally. When she behaves that way, she is simply being a teenager. Your responsibility is to be a parent and remain in control. This phase will soon pass, if you continue to love her unconditionally and hold her accountable for her behavior. If your teenager is putting herself and the rest of the family at risk, it is important that you clearly spell out the consequences of certain behaviors and be consistent with having her suffer the consequences by losing privileges that she thoroughly enjoys.

Trust God for patience and wisdom to weather the storms of raising teenagers. We will continue to pray for you and hope you will pray for us as we strive to do our best with the teenagers God has placed in our care.

Parenting Woes

My thirteen-year-old daughter feels that the boundaries we have set for her are too strict. She told my husband and me that we are the meanest parents in town. When we try to be more flexible, she still doesn't appreciate it. How do we set clear boundaries and still keep a peaceful home?

Congratulations. You are now officially on the roller-coaster ride of teenage parenting. Hold on tight, try to grin through your pain and fear, and pray that you will get through this in one piece. With God's grace and help you will.

Knowing how firm or how flexible to be with our children is one of the most difficult tasks of parenting. However, if parents do not set boundaries, kids will make up their own, often to their harm. Even the youngest of children will try to call the shots in the home. Teenagers are definitely no exception. Often parents fear that if they set boundaries their children will feel unloved. Not true. Children feel most loved when there is a sense of safety and security. It is important for you as parents to establish, consistently and lovingly, that you are the ones in charge in your home. This does not mean that you will be dictators, but it means that you will exert loving leadership while nurturing your children.

When setting boundaries, do so based on principle. Do not be afraid to be flexible on the things that are not of most importance, but stand firm on the values that are nonnegotiable to your family, especially character issues. Sit down with your daughter and establish what is acceptable and what is not. Allow her to voice her opinions and say why she does or does not agree. Whether she understands or not at this point, there are boundaries that should remain in place because as parents you think it best.

Do not become overly concerned about your daughter's outbursts of anger. As painful as it may be, try not to take her words of outrage too seriously or personally, and expect that she will always have strong feelings when her own way is being challenged. Encourage her to express her anger, as long as it is done in a respectful and civil way. You are the responsible adults in this relationship, and your daughter is becoming all that you and God want her to be.

Raising teenagers will help us come to an even deeper understanding of God's love for us, since we often behave as difficult teens with God.

And yet He promises to love us with an everlasting love. So even as you are setting boundaries, remember to love lavishly. This is the time our children need to be reassured of our love. The boundaries will provide the security. The hugs and kisses—even when we don't feel like it at times—will reassure them of our love.

"And this is my prayer: that your love may abound more and more in knowledge and depth of insight, so that you may be able to discern what is best" (Philippians 1:9, 10, NIV).

Parenting Not for the Faint of Heart

Being a parent has turned out to be the most difficult thing I've ever done. I don't want to hurt my children, but I get very tired of going over and over and over the same stuff every day. Do you have any suggestions that truly work in real life?

We immediately identify with your statement about parenting being most difficult. We have two children—eleven and fourteen—and have often felt as frustrated as you sound. However, there are skills that almost any parent can learn, if she or he is willing to accept them.

The purpose of parenting is to share one's values with one's children, to share one's concept of God. We are called to share our perception of right and wrong, honesty and truthfulness, privilege and responsibility. After all, we aim to raise children who are happy, healthy, confident, cooperative, and responsible. We also aim to develop a healthy, lifelong relationship with our children that will help them grow to be responsible and loving adults.

In order to raise great kids, there are two questions you should ask yourself: First, what do you like about what you are currently doing as a parent? Second, what are you currently doing that you would like to change?

There are at least three major styles of parenting: (1) giving orders (authoritarian); (2) giving in (permissive); (3) giving choices (democratic).

Authoritarian parents are strict. They set a lot of rules. Children are expected to obey the rules exactly as they are given. And often children are punished or rewarded so that they may be controlled. In this style of parenting, children expect a reward for "being good."

Consequently, children may follow strict rules to avoid being punished or "getting into trouble." Children may also learn to be afraid of parents. They may not learn to think for themselves. Rather, they will look to friends and peers to tell them what to do and may not always get good advice.

Authoritarian parents often yell, blame, or hit children. To regain a sense of control, children may copy the behavior of parents when dealing with siblings or peers by yelling or being violent to solve their problems. Of course, children need to trust their parents, not fear them. They also need to see that calm words, not yelling or hitting, is the way to work out problems.

Permissive parents simply set no limits and often change the limits they have set. Indeed, children who are parented this way grow up without consistent boundaries, since parents usually give in to whatever their children want. However, freedom without limits usually means problems for everyone, because our society is characterized by boundaries.

Children who have not learned proper boundaries will have trouble knowing how to behave in our society.

As a matter of fact, having no boundaries causes insecurity in children. It is like driving without any rules or laws. The results would be devastating, and we wouldn't even be able to call them accidents.

Democratic parents are neither permissive nor authoritarian. Democratic parents balance freedom (privileges) and limits (responsibilities). This approach helps children become responsible by teaching them to set limits and provides choices within those limits. This approach teaches children that every privilege has a corresponding responsibility. Democratic parents stimulate their children to make some decisions on their own.

In order to maximize the benefits of democratic parenting, parents should be sure that the choices they are offering are choices they can accept. The choices given to children should also match their age and maturity. For example, if your thirteen-year-old loves to play basketball whenever she gets a chance, you may say, "You may play basketball before dinner as long as your homework is completed and ready for school the following day." It is quite simple. If homework is not ready before dinner, it means that she has chosen not to play basketball that day. The onus is on your daughter to determine whether basketball will be a part of her day or not.

Allowing your children to have a right to their own likes and dislikes is called differentiation. When differentiation is allowed to exist, all members of a family don't need to have the same taste in sneakers, shirts, music, or ties—only in being loved, respected, and regarded.

When children are allowed to choose and participate in decision-making, they learn that their choices count. They also learn that choices carry responsibility.

Coping After Divorce

I've just been through a divorce, and I hate to see what it is doing to my children, who are nine and eleven years old. What can I do to help them cope?

First of all, we are terribly sorry to hear about your divorce. Divorce is truly a traumatic experience for most and a devastating experience for many. Please be sure that you and your family will be in our prayers.

While a large number of family therapists, counselors, and family researchers agree—and so do we—that divorce adversely affects the lives of children, parents can weigh in to help make the pain less severe. Therefore, your question is a valuable one.

Since you stated that you have "just been through a divorce," we will deal only with the first stage of divorce, which is known as the *immediate crisis* phase. While for some families the first stage may last for a month or two after the parents physically separate, for other families that stage may go on for a year or two past the point of separation. The length of this phase depends on how much effort the divorcing parents put into being civil to each other for the sake of their children's emotional well-being.

Parents can help their children through this first stage of the divorce by sharing with them their decision to divorce—prior to the event—in order to prepare them for it. The custodial parent needs to be mindful of the emotional pain being experienced by their children, empathizing with them and allowing them to talk about their feelings in an open and honest way. Parents should stay away from criticizing the other parent, or using their children to pry into the private life of the other parent. Also, be aware that your children are dealing with conflicting emotions.

Children will also engage in a range of common psychological defenses, such as being unemotional about upsetting matters, teasing or fighting with siblings and peers, having headaches or stomachaches, becoming overly devoted to one parent, and identifying with the absent parent. Parents should be careful not to confront these matters directly, since that would serve no useful end.

A much better way to relate to this behavior is by speaking to your children indirectly. For example, if your son is getting into trouble at school, you may say: "Sometimes guys have pretty hurt feelings when their parents are divorcing, and take them out on their classmates by fighting with them."

For more information, read Neil Kalter, *Growing Up With Divorce: Helping Your Child Avoid Immediate and Later Emotional Problems* (New York: Free Press, 1990).

Judith S. Wallerstein, Julia M. Lewis, and Sandra Blakeslee, *The Unexpected Legacy of Divorce: A 25-Year Landmark Study* (New York: Hyperion, 2000).

Single Mother Raising a Son

I am the single mother of three children, one of them a boy who has just turned thirteen, and I simply don't know what to do with him. My husband and I divorced several years ago, and since he remarried about three years ago he has made no effort to see our children. The three children are hurt, but my son is taking it especially hard and often tells me he doesn't want to talk with me because I don't understand "men things." Please recommend something I can do to help my son.

Single parenting is among the most difficult relationships to manage. Whether one is a single parent through divorce, death, or by not being married to the father or mother of one's child or children, it is obvious that there are things one simply cannot do.

One clear reason for God's family ideal of mother and father to be coparents is that there are things only men can give to children, and there are things that only women can give to children.

Our comments are not meant to add to your concerns, but to make you aware of a natural vacuum that takes place when children are raised with only one parent.

Although modern Western societies have elevated the nuclear family (father, mother, and children) as the ideal, most people around the world have historically employed successfully the model of the extended family to help them rear their children and manage multiple household tasks.

Every single parent needs the help of a role model who is of the opposite sex. Boys being raised by their mothers are in particular need of a male role model, especially if they are going through the challenges of being a teen.

It is no criticism of any mother that there are some subjects her teenage son would feel more comfortable talking over with another male. And it is just as important for daughters to identify with a healthy and consistent male role model.

This is a great opportunity to introduce what is called para-parents into the single-parent family unit, so that boys and girls can have a feel for how husbands and wives, men and women, as well as sons and daughters, behave with one another.

We would suggest that you be intentional about recruiting such help for your children, and especially for your son at this time. Rather than simply finding one of your brothers, which is often helpful, or a male at church to mentor your son, a less risky proposition is to recruit a couple, or even a family at church, among your friends and/or relatives who is willing to become a part of your family through these crucial years with your children.

Para-parents may attend church with your family; participate in home Bible studies or worship with your family; share potlucks; and provide friendship, companionship, and support—provided there is a clear understanding of their role and what the family has decided to offer your family. Be sure to show your appreciation to the family you have adopted or who has adopted you. Do not be jealous if your children make comparisons.

As Christians we should remember that if God is our Father, then we are brothers and sisters, which means that we all belong to the same family. We hope this helps you with your need to reach your son right now. Please know that we are praying for you.

Selected Bibliography

Dating

National Marriage Project. *The State of Our Unions: Marriage in America, 2012.* Charlottesville, VA: University of Virginia, 2012.

Waite, Linda J., and Maggie Gallagher. *The Case for Marriage: Why Married People Are Happier, Healthier, and Better Off Financially.* New York: Doubleday, 2000.

Weiner-Davis, Michele. *The Divorce Remedy: The Proven 7-Step Program for Saving Your Marriage.* New York: Simon and Schuster, 2002.

Infidelity

Laaser, Mark and Debra. *The Seven Desires of Every Heart.* Grand Rapids, MI: Zondervan, 2008.

Leman, Kevin. *Sheet Music: Uncovering the Secrets of Sexual Intimacy in Marriage.* Carol Stream, IL: Tyndale House Publishers, 2003.